DIRTBAG,
MASSACHUSETTS

DIRTBAG, MASSACHUSETTS

A CONFESSIONAL

ISAAC FITZGERALD

BLOOMSBURY PUBLISHING

NEW YORK · LONDON · OXFORD · NEW DELHI · SYDNEY

BLOOMSBURY PUBLISHING
Bloomsbury Publishing Inc.
1385 Broadway, New York, NY 10018, USA

BLOOMSBURY, BLOOMSBURY PUBLISHING, and the Diana logo
are trademarks of Bloomsbury Publishing Plc

First published in the United States 2022

Although this is a work of nonfiction, the author has changed the names of
certain individuals to protect their privacy and has reconstructed dialogue to
the best of his recollection.

LIBRARY OF CONGRESS CATALOGING-IN-PUBLICATION DATA IS AVAILABLE

ISBN: HB: 978-1-63557-397-8; EBOOK: 978-1-63557-398-5

2 4 6 8 10 9 7 5 3 1

Typeset by Westchester Publishing Services
Printed and bound in the U.S.A.

To find out more about our authors and books visit www.bloomsbury.com
and sign up for our newsletters.

Bloomsbury books may be purchased for business or promotional use. For
information on bulk purchases please contact Macmillan Corporate and
Premium Sales Department at specialmarkets@macmillan.com.

For my family, both chosen and those who didn't have a choice

When stray dogs finally catch you in the alley,
You don't consider their point of view
But when the wounds are healed, and the scars are shiny,
Sometimes, then, you do
—John Darnielle, "As Many Candles as Possible"

CONTENTS

Family Stories

My parents were married when they had me, just to different people.

That's the way I open every story when I'm asked about my childhood. I was a child of passion! A happy little accident. Or, put another way, I was born of sin: a mistake in human form, a bomb aimed perfectly to blow up both my parents' lives.

MY MOTHER GREW up in a big old red house in North Central Massachusetts: a hill town surrounded by river towns, all of them now emptied of hill people and river people, their main streets boarded up after most of the industrial jobs moved down south, before moving out of the country entirely.

The house dated back to the 1700s, set on a farm on an ancient turnpike. My mother grew up there among sheep and chickens and geese and even a few horses and a goat, her parents flinty and unforgiving people who loved the land. My mother worked hard, went to a respectable college in Maine, married a Unitarian minister. They had a little boy, Joel. Her life was idyllic, apart from the restlessness in her heart.

My father was born to mill workers in New Bedford, Massachusetts. In the 1800s the town had been one of the world's largest and most important whaling ports. Melville mentioned it in the opening pages of *Moby-Dick*. You can still visit the Seamen's Bethel today and admire its bow-shaped pulpit. You should know, however, that the church installed it only *after Moby-Dick* was published—the image an invention of Melville's—and that the novel itself was mostly written far from the sea, closer to where my mother grew up, in the whale-shaped hills of Pittsfield, Massachusetts.

My mother's family didn't have much, and my father's family had less. New Bedford, like any good fishing port, was a rough town back then, and when he was growing up my father made trouble the way children in rough towns do, but he was also the first of his family to go to college, after which he got a job selling textbooks and eventually married his high school girlfriend. They had a daughter, Kerry.

My parents' lives mirrored one another's in many ways—both had married their high school sweethearts; both had kids already; both had nice lives that they could have kept on living until they died. Both were smart, itchy, unsteady people who had read too many books, if such a thing is possible, and I'm pretty sure it is.

When the whaling industry began to fall apart, many of the whalers moved west to California, hoping to find their fortune. I mention this only because before they met each other, both of my parents did the same: moved to California, looking for a better life. But both returned to the East Coast without discovering whatever kind of gold it was that they'd been seeking. Years later, believing I was the first in my family to do so, I would do the same. Only to find that in an attempt to escape my parents' shadows I had simply been following their stained and tattered map.

MY PARENTS MET at divinity school, which is a pretty funny way to start an affair. I could add that to the story next time I tell it, although it's also not funny, especially to my parents. Divinity school wasn't a joke to them. They entered as two separate people, both in their thirties, confused and lonely and searching for some kind of salvation—but they wanted to find it the hard way.

They met in an Old Testament class taught by an older professor named Dr. Holladay—I called him "Doc Holliday," like the cowboy—with whom they would eventually end up living when I was a baby when they had no home to call their own and zero support from their families—my father's having none to give and my mother's so disapproving that they chose to withhold it all.

I believe it was my mother's only affair. I know it wasn't my father's. They would tell their spouses they were going on spiritual retreats—then abscond to the White Mountains in New Hampshire to spend time with one another, camping to save money.

My mother would eventually break it off. She had a son and a husband with a good job and a house. A family. The beginnings of a life. This was just a panic fling, she told herself: one final push against the life that was expected of her before she settled down.

My father, not new to this game, talked my mother into one last trip to the mountains.

In what can only be described as the dictionary definition of TMI, I know that both my parents were using birth control during this trip and that despite their precautionary measures I was conceived on top of a mountain. Mount Carrigain. I know this because my mother told me. Telling a child at a very young age, whom you're raising in the Catholic Church, that he was a miracle conception is a choice. Messy parenting, maybe, but it makes for another good story.

MY MOTHER DEBATED telling her husband that I was his. She didn't know what to do—she and my father had broken up, after all, and he was predominantly out of the picture.

On the cover of my baby book the name WILLIAM ISAAC HELLEN is lovingly embroidered in red cloth letters onto dark-blue patterned fabric. The first name for my father, the middle name for me, and the last my mother's maiden name. My whole life has been spent with teachers and officials asking, "William . . . do you prefer Bill? Or Will? Or . . ." "Isaac," I'd respond to their surprise. And then add breezily, "My mother didn't understand first names."

EVENTUALLY MY FATHER came back on the scene, his wife having grown weary of his infidelities. After a year living with the kindly Dr. Holladay in his cramped apartment, our little trio finally landed at the Catholic Worker, a socialist Catholic charity that housed the homeless and fed the hungry. Soon my parents were a part of their community, and so was I. We were living in the South End of Boston, first on Dartmouth Street when I was a baby, then on Tremont Street as a toddler, and finally at John Leary House—a low-income apartment building run by the Catholic Worker on Massachusetts Avenue. It was called Mass Ave for short, and as a child, I used to think our street was named after a church service, not the state we lived in.

I loved those early years. I loved growing up in Boston. My father would go running along the Charles River, as I biked beside him, pumping my little legs in an attempt to keep up. Or he'd take me to Fenway Park. This was the eighties, before the Sox were a winning team and before Fenway was almost constantly sold out. My dad would buy standing-room tickets, the cheapest you could get. Come the second or third inning, he'd have us in seats down by the field, so close you could smell the grass. Sometimes the seats belonged to season ticket holders who hadn't shown up; sometimes they were just empty. But if the ticket holders ever did arrive, or security got curious, my pa would turn and say, "Oh, I'm very sorry. It's just that the seats were open and, well, it's my son's first game." We almost always got to stay in our seats, or would sometimes be ushered to even better ones.

I must have had a hundred first games.

I LOVED HANGING out in the soup kitchen, too. Haley House. I was surrounded by all sorts of people there, people just like me, or people not like me; from various walks of life; but because we were at the soup kitchen together we *were* like each other; we shared something important. Community. I was surrounded by stories of the highest comedy and the deepest tragedy, by the sounds of pealing laughter and suffering silence. I didn't know my experience was any different from the way other children grew up. I was poor but cared for; back then my parents were good to each other and to me, and nobody told me I was supposed to be miserable. I was taught magic tricks that were more like street hustles than anything you'd do with a top hat and wand—tricks that trained you to ignore the patter and the dazzle and keep your eye on the cards, searching for the sleight of hand.

One Haley House regular taught me bar tricks I'd use later in life, demonstrating them to me with the small glasses meant for communion, filling them with apple juice instead of whiskey.

"I bet I can drink these two big glasses before you can drink those two small glasses."

"No you can't!" I'd respond, even though I already knew the trick.

"It'll be hard, but I can do it. Give me a little head start: I'll drink this big glass first and then you can try to drink those two little glasses before I finish the second big glass. But there's just one rule: You're not allowed to touch each other's glasses. That way nobody can cheat. Okay?"

"Okay," I'd agree. I watched as he chugged the first big glass. The moment he finished it, my hand darted out to reach for my first little shot of apple juice, which I quickly drank. But before I could pick up my second shot, he placed his first empty glass upside down over my second little glass. Then he slowly sipped his second drink, savoring every drop and smiling as I laughed and tried to figure out a way to remove his glass without touching it.

EVEN BEFORE I learned how to read I learned to respect books as a second religion. My parents' faith in literature was as strong as their faith in Catholicism; maybe stronger. No matter what else we didn't—couldn't—have, my parents surrounded us with books. Our apartment was bare save for milk crates overflowing with novels and plays and history books and collections of Shakespeare and, of course, the Bible. Stories matter to my family. My earliest memories are of my parents reading to me. Every time we moved, they always left our hand-me-down chairs and rickety tables on the curb, knowing they could get cheap furniture elsewhere. But the books were packed away in boxes and stuffed into whatever old, rusted car the family was driving that year.

Your parents' obsessions can so often become your obsessions, especially if your parents themselves are hard to hold. I fell in love with the idea of adventure after my father read me *The Hobbit* at five. I fell in love with and also gained a deep respect for the sea after he read me "The Rime of the Ancient Mariner"—not to mention an almost ridiculous fear of seagulls when he failed to explain that an albatross was a completely different type of bird.

Even from a young (too young?) age, I knew what a great opening line I had in "My parents were married when they had me, just to different people." I had been read so many books, heard so many opening lines, that those were the shapes I thought and spoke in. Everything was books; or no, wait, everything was stories.

IN MY STORY of my family, everything went to shit when I turned eight years old. Happy to sad, light to dark, together to apart. The stark divide of it in my memory makes me think of Sara Crewe, the heroine of Frances Hodgson Burnett's *A Little Princess*, who is having an incredibly baller birthday celebration at her boarding school when the headmistress receives word that her heretofore-rich colonizer father has died and left Sara penniless. The headmistress goes *yoink!* "Party's over, give me your stuff, here's a burlap smock to wear while you work as an unpaid servant at the school you attended until just two seconds ago."

Maybe it wasn't that sudden for me. But when our lives changed, it had hinged on one decision: My parents decided that city life was no longer for them. I had gotten mugged at gunpoint around the corner from where we lived (I wasn't hurt and the mugger apologized to me when he saw that I'd peed my pants), and a man had recently been shot on our apartment building's front stoop while we were asleep in our beds, the dried blood still visible the next day. But whatever the reason, my parents believed that the solution lay in blowing up their lives yet again.

While my father stayed in Boston for the time being, my mother and I moved to the small rural town in North Central Massachusetts where she had grown up. We lived in a gray house right next door to my grandmother's big red one. My mother's mother, who still could not believe or accept what my mother had done to her life. Whose disapproval and anger was powerful enough to spread far and cloak both houses.

I'M SURE THE move looked like an appealing next chapter to my parents. Running away from the "dirty and dangerous" city to the "fresh and unspoiled" countryside. It just sounds appealing—romantic, even. Yet it all turned out so horribly that I still can't believe they didn't read the warning signs. That it might be a bad idea for a married couple to endure long periods of separation, especially when one of them had previous issues with monogamy. That it might be a bad idea for a daughter to move next door to her harsh and judgmental mother, whom she'd been lucky enough to escape once already, with her bastard child in tow. That it might be a bad idea for a mother and son, accustomed to living in a city around people and life and heat and voices, to uproot themselves and move into the woods, and its silence.

Each time I retell this story, I feel the urge to stop it. Like shouting at a horror movie. *Don't go down into the basement. Don't go. Don't.*

THOUGH WE MOVED, we brought our poverty with us. We went from city poor to country poor. In the gray house, the paint was chipped and the rooms drafty. A large cast-iron stove sat at the center of the house, which we used to heat ourselves, and also the bricks we'd bring up to warm our freezing beds. Out in the backyard was a rusted-out water pump that froze in the winter, as did our clothes that we hung on the line.

I missed my father the way you miss something you don't know is missing, which is to say I didn't know why he was gone. I could feel the trouble but I couldn't put words to it. Meanwhile, my mother cried herself to sleep most nights, asked me to stay in bed with her some nights, and spoke to me more like a friend she could confide in than the child I was.

Because of this, I began to treasure my private time. My deep loneliness transmuting into something else, but something related—an aloneness. I was changing. I came to love those hours each day when my mother was at work, teaching at an elementary school many miles away, and I had the house, my whole life, to myself. Living at the edge of town, I was the first child picked up on the bus route every morning and the last one dropped off every afternoon. Walking a half a mile to the end of our road, I often popped into the woods to smoke a cigarette, a bottle of stolen cologne hidden in the knot of a tree nearby, as if spraying it would cover anything up.

My bus driver was a wise woman named Trudy who would pretend not to notice the tears on mornings when my mother's sadness managed to work its way into my heart, who was well aware that whatever was going on in my home wasn't good. Trudy never pushed, was never obvious, but would say something light, something comforting. I didn't have to ask for her reassurances, and I never would have asked for them. Trudy just knew.

ALMOST IMMEDIATELY AFTER my mother and I moved to the country, my father had an affair in the city. An affair my mother would come to know about and which proved everything her parents had said was true. An affair that would wreck her, and us.

But they stayed together. Eventually, my father was able to leave the city and reunite the family, living next to the in-laws who hated him even more than they hated me and my mother's choices. Then I learned about my father's anger. And I learned that these things—her sadness, his anger—were mine as well. Life at home got so hard that trying to make everything better, trying to hide away, was impossible. Instead, I claimed my inheritances.

WHEN I WAS eight, my mother told me that she had almost aborted me. The sun was shining, and we were driving in her beat-up white Toyota Corolla station wagon on the one road that went to the center of town. We'd been living in the gray house for just a few months; my father hadn't yet come to join us.

The heat rose off the small highway in waves, making it look like the asphalt was covered in water. I was wondering what made that happen—a very eight-year-old thing to wonder—when she suddenly spoke the words aloud.

The still, humid air in the car hung between us as we crawled up the crest of a hill, the engine noisy with lack of oil. I concentrated on the heat shimmer ahead, hoping that the conversation was already over.

"Maybe it would have been for the best," she said. And then, as they always did, more words spilled out of her.

I didn't react. I just stared at the glistening blacktop, wishing the waves were real and the water below so deep it could swallow up the entire car, taking us along with it.

My mother was sick. She was in a desperate place. She told me too much about the eight years of my life and how they came about, as if it were a way to pass the time, to keep her madness at bay. She would talk and talk, and I would listen, probably more than she realized. Letting it all pour into me. All these family stories.

I divide my life into two time periods. There is before eight, and then there is everything that came after. There is before my mother told me she almost aborted me and then there is everything that followed. My mother had yet to reach the bottom of her sadness. The violence of my father hadn't yet crept into our house. The coming decade stretched long and terrible in front of us.

"Maybe it would have been for the best."

The car drove over the shimmering asphalt. We didn't sink into the water but continued down the road. Crashing into whatever would come next.

Forgive Me

The confessional booth felt like every other confessional booth I'd ever been in. The wood of the bench was so dark and uniformly grained that it looked fake, and the once-plush cushion atop it was now dingy and flat. Between me and the priest was a metal lattice that transformed people into murky, anonymous silhouettes.

"What did her hair smell like?"

I didn't like not being able to see the priest—maybe because he was more fearsome as a disembodied voice, more powerful, which is to say that maybe what I didn't like was being put in the position of a supplicant—but at least there was a barrier between us.

"Son?"

I was twelve and at a church in Boston with my parents. Though we had moved to rural Massachusetts a few years earlier, the three of us still returned to the city now and then to visit our friends at the Catholic Worker.

In so many ways, my family had barely survived the move. My parents had hoped that living in the country would bring us space, peace, safety, closeness. Instead what we got was lone-liness, depression, anger, disconnection. But we stuck it out, or they did (as a child I didn't have much of a choice), and after those terrible first years, my parents were getting better—my mother no longer so despairing, my father no longer ragingly loud or frighteningly silent. Meanwhile, I got worse.

So, at the beginning of confession, I told the priest about breaking into houses to raid liquor cabinets, lifting bottles from package stores and cigarettes from grocery stores, trading bottles and cigarettes for weed and mushrooms. My parents were sober, my father a recovering alcoholic and my mother choosing to join him in his sobriety; there were no bottles to steal in our home. I confessed to sneaking out of the house and riding in the backs of trucks as my older friends pushed the pedal into the floor and whipped around back roads, my body almost bouncing out into the night. I did not trust my parents, so I thought it only fair that I was worthy of their distrust as well. The priest nodded and listened and let my confes-sions crash against him and then wash away.

Until I mentioned Ashley.

Here the looming silhouette straightened. "Go on," the priest said.

No, I did not want to confess what Ashley and I had done recently in a forest behind a friend's house in the rural hills of Massachusetts. However, I was pretty sure that not wanting to confess something meant that you really should, and after boring him with all the exploits I'd been vaguely proud-ashamed of, I was glad to finally have the priest's full attention, although there was already something too avid and alert about his ear.

So I used my words to tell him the story of what Ashley and I had done. We had gotten drunk off a few warm, stolen beers in the way only kids can get drunk, and we had gotten high off a poorly rolled joint, which a group of us had shared while drinking Walmart-brand Dr Pepper. Ashley and I had split off from our friends. We were alone together. She was seventeen. We kissed and we touched and we rolled around in the dirt and the wet leaves and slowly she put me in her mouth and even more slowly I lay there pretending to understand what was happening but knowing that I liked it. Her hair smelled like blackberries, but fake. Like an ad for blackberries.

I told him about the leaves and the priest asked for more. I described her knuckles pressing into my stomach as she undid my belt and he asked for more. I described how her body felt against mine. His breath seemed to fill the confessional.

Ashley had said, after she was finished, that she could tell I wasn't old enough yet. "You lasted too long," she said. Later in life I would know what she meant, but at the time I was only confused.

In that moment I remembered her words. *This is lasting too long.* The priest had heard all my sins with no questions, no requests for me to elaborate. Not until Ashley. Then he kept asking and asking and asking. I answered his questions about her. Until he asked, "What did it feel like? In her mouth." And after I was silent.

"What did her hair smell like?" "Son?"

The low light of candles filled the darkness of the confessional booth as I opened the door and stumbled into the empty nave, through the pews and out the door into the waning daylight. My parents were waiting on the front steps.

My father looked at me. "Had a lot to confess?" Like I said, my parents were getting better. I was getting worse. He wasn't blind. I shrugged and walked ahead of them. Away from the church.

WHEN I WAS six years old and we were still living in Boston, the Catholic Worker had gotten my ma a new job, at the Cathedral of the Holy Cross, which was and is the cathedral of the Roman Catholic archdiocese of Boston and one of the largest Roman Catholic churches in New England. They needed a lot of help, so my ma became, essentially, the personal assistant to the cathedral itself. She cleaned and tidied, pitched in with secretarial duties, and assisted the priests.

From the outside, the church is a stone behemoth standing guard over the neighborhood, offering both protection and judgment. It served a large, mostly Irish American congregation, almost everyone immigrants or the children of immigrants, while also serving a new growing immigrant community with Spanish-language services during the off-hours, usually in the smaller chapel, which was always jam-packed with congregants. I remember sneaking in to listen to those services, where the psalms were sung in a language I didn't know yet felt both familiar and elusive, like a dream I'd almost forgotten. But the incense always smelled the same.

My ma had told me that the cathedral was supposed to have a grand spire. Instead, there is a big tower stretching up into the sky until it suddenly stops short and squares off, like a partially completed homework assignment. You can almost feel a strange sort of tension and possibility in the air above, as if at any moment a spire still might fall magically from the sky to fill the emptiness.

When I told my ma that, I remember her laughing, a certain low and gently rueful laugh she's had her whole life, which I'm sure was appreciated by the Cathedral priests and anyone else who has ever needed to hear a laugh perfect for when things are so hopeless that they're also a little bit funny.

"More likely they ran out of money," she had answered, touching the back of my head as we walked up toward the gray stone castle. "Everybody in this neighborhood does." I didn't get the joke then, but now I do.

When you walk into the nave, everything opens up and the inside seems even bigger than the outside, somehow. It would feel massive to anyone at any age, but when you're six and enveloped by the shadow of the enormous organ as you follow its countless pipes reaching up and up and up to a ceiling so far away it might as well be the sky, it was so deeply lonely and self-abnegating that it was almost transcendental.

While my ma was working I'd often hide among the endless pews, decipher the stories told through the stained-glass windows, or circle around the perimeter of the nave, my own endlessly looping rendition of the stations of the cross. I would hide in the confessionals and sometimes just find a corner and flip through the hymnals, trying to sound out the words and not even trying with the musical notes, which were all unsolvable math to me. Sometimes I would play in the cathedral until after the sun went down, the figures in the stained glass gradually losing whatever spark of life they'd been granted by the sun shining through them, taking on an air of menace as they dimmed.

The priests quickly noticed that my ma was good at her job and dependable, so they started giving her more responsibility, bigger tasks, and more complex, longer-term projects. Eventually, she was working with Cardinal Bernard Francis Law, the archbishop of Boston, himself. Despite not being from Boston, he had one of those big slabby Boston faces, with kindly but piercing eyes, topped with a full head of white hair. He wasn't exactly handsome, but given his line of work, his avuncular, warmly intelligent, *trustworthy* vibe was better than handsome, and far more useful. You could understand why people followed him, listened to him. Believed in him. Here was a man who certainly must have the ear of God.

Cardinal Law was also quick to smile, when he wasn't performing mass for the congregation, and was always friendly to me when I was around. He grinned when I insisted on calling him "Blue Jay Law" instead of "Cardinal Law," certainly one of the funniest bird jokes that had ever been told, while my mother tried to shoo me away, anxious about keeping this new and much-needed job (one that had both the downside and benefit of enraging her Protestant parents). But even as a six-year-old I understood that he was an Influential Man who was important to my mother's happiness, so I disobeyed and hammed it up even more. It isn't every day that you get to put a smile on the face of a man who talks directly to God.

My half-brother, Joel, lived in Newton with his dad, a Unitarian minister. Sometimes Joel would come visit, and if something came up at the church during the weekend, my ma would have to take us both to work with her. We would often hang out in the rectory, a comfy building but one that lacked any of the magic of the cathedral. This was where the priests actually had to *live* in between performing their ceremonial and spiritual (not to mention administrative) roles, and where I had always felt welcome to hang around, even without Joel, sometimes whiling away hours on a couch there, watching television with whoever was around.

Different priests were always coming and going. They visited from other parts of Massachusetts or New England, in Boston for meetings or special services, or they came to live in the city while they waited to get transferred to another parish somewhere in the surrounding area. In the rectory, the grand tableaux of suffering and sacrifice, told in gold and dark polished wood and every shade of glass, was put aside for half-full ashtrays and bulky furniture upholstered in something green and plastic that didn't even try to mimic an animal's hide. In these more informal quarters, the priests exchanged their ceremonial garb for a plain black suit of clothes finished with a white plastic collar, but sometimes even those would be dispensed with, their shirts left unbuttoned at the top. Strangest and most uncomfortable of all for a young child not sure what to make of it was when the priests simply wore laymen's clothes and looked too much like any other person.

I looked up to Joel for a lot of reasons, for being my half-brother, for being four years older than me, for being more physically active and adventurous and better at sports than I ever was. But especially because we both liked books. I loved to hear Joel read from the Encyclopedia Brown series, even though he was almost always able to guess the correct solutions while I, with a kind of optimistic helplessness, just made up ones based on imaginary clues that hadn't even been in the story. ("A chipmunk stole it!")

That's where the idea for the Half-Brothers Detective Agency came from. We didn't really know what "half-brother" meant, but, at least for me, it made me feel special. As if the phrase meant something *more* than brothers because it took two words to say, even though one of those words was "half."

When our ma had been called into work again, we parked ourselves in the rectory and made a sign advertising the Half-Brothers Detective Agency, folding the paper so it stood on its own on the laminate table top (green and plastic, like everything else), the sign boldly proclaiming that our agency could solve ANY crime. A few priests walked by and kidded with us without lingering before one came into the kitchen and leaned against the counter to read the sign, a grin already spreading across his face.

"Any crime, huh?" he said.

"That's right, Father," I said, looking at Joel. "My brother is smarter than Encyclopedia Brown."

The priest laughed. "Well, then I'm in luck. Because my wife has gone missing."

I looked at my brother again. I knew priests couldn't have wives, but did my Unitarian half-brother know that? Joel didn't return my look. He was already on the case, peppering the priest with questions. When was she last seen? Was there anywhere she might have gone? I couldn't tell what Joel was thinking, but I followed his lead. Maybe this would be the case that I finally got to solve, instead of him.

Meanwhile, the priest was saying, "No, she wouldn't be in my room . . . but I do know she's still in the building. And don't forget, she's extremely fat."

I had obviously missed some clues while zoning out, so I did my best to refocus.

Joel was frowning a little, deep in thought. Then his eyes lit up. "What about . . . Is there an attic here?"

The priest's smile widened. "There is! Hmm, my wife *might* be too fat to fit in the attic, but let's go check, shall we?"

We got to the attic by pulling down a stepladder. The attic was full of sunlight, hazy with dust. Though it was used for storage and there was a lot of turnover due to the number of priests coming and going, things looked surprisingly orderly. Dust there was, but no cobwebs.

My memory of this part is a little indistinct, probably because something extremely memorable happened right after. The priest pretended that we had indeed found his fat wife in the attic—I don't remember how Joel and I dealt with the fact that there was clearly no one else up there—and gave us some hard candies as our reward.

I snuck mine into my pocket, like my ma had taught me during our time at Haley House, the homeless shelter, where the other residents had fascinated me. I'd often goof off and try to make them laugh while they slurped soup and chewed bread with gap-filled mouths, sitting under a big sign that read NO ALCOHOL. NO DRUGS. NO VIOLENCE. Sometimes I'd annoy some of the residents so much that they'd shout at me, unless they were so hungover that all they could do was scowl. Other times, they laughed and played along. An old man named Albert always called me "Captain" and often gave me butterscotch candies as a reward for the entertainment I'd provided. Then my ma got wind of it and took me aside, opening her hand to show me a butterscotch candy so ancient that tiny white worms had bored into it. She explained to me that Albert lived alone and had no one around to tell him when he should throw away and replace things, so his butterscotch candies were very old, like he was, and the next time anyone at the homeless shelter gave me *anything*, the proper thing to do was to thank the person very nicely, and then put the candy or whatever in my pocket to bring to her right away. Of course my mother never would have thought to worry about telling me what to do with candy from a priest. Why would she have had to?

Suddenly, a harsh voice blared behind us. "What are you doing up here?" Another priest had climbed up to the attic, this one short, compactly built, all furrows and radiating anger. "You are not allowed up here!"

The first priest turned red. "We were just joking around," he said, addressing him by a name I've completely forgotten, washed away as it was by the surreal shock of hearing a priest called by his first name.

Joel tried to smooth things over by explaining about our detective agency, but the angry priest cut him off, ignoring him to lock eyes with me. "Isaac," he said.

Uh-oh. I didn't recognize him, but he clearly recognized me.

He continued, speaking so emphatically that each word was a self-contained monument to his fury. "Where. Is. Your. Mother?"

The friendly priest slipped away, retreating down the attic stairs without even a goodbye, and the mean priest marched us through the rectory until Joel and I found our mother. We were told to sit on a long red couch, a detail I remember mainly because I am surprised it wasn't green, and pretended not to listen to the heated yell-whispers coming from the other room. We couldn't hear much in the way of specific words but the way they sounded told us plenty.

Somehow, we had really messed up.

My mother's job was crucial to her. It was crucial to the whole family—for one thing, we desperately needed the money—but it meant even more to her. She liked that she was good at it; she liked that she had proven herself and risen quickly and that her hard work and great intelligence had been rewarded, which was something that did not happen nearly as often as she deserved. I knew ma didn't like all the priests she dealt with, but overall her job made her happy and proud, and I felt deeply ashamed that we had jeopardized it with our silly detective agency. I looked at my brother and he looked at the floor so I looked at the floor too.

The mean priest and my mother walked back into the room. Now he looked only stern, not all furious and scary like before, but I still hated him. I hated that he had yelled, albeit quietly, at my mother, and I hated that he had gotten so upset over what had clearly been a game. It was bewildering; it was unfair. The other priest had wanted only to be kind and entertain two kids while their mother was working. Playful and harmless—a made-up wife, a case to solve, a sunlit attic, and hard candies. He didn't deserve to be yelled at, and neither did we, and neither did my mom, by this strict, heartless priest who seemed to hate fun and love enforcing rules no one else knew.

As we left, he said one last thing. "You can't keep bringing your boys here, Susan. This is not a place for children."

On the walk home our mother called the priest a "prick." I didn't know what the word meant but I could tell by the way it sounded and the way she said it that I agreed. The man was *clearly* a prick. Ma was a working mother who often had to do her job while trying to care for one, sometimes two, sometimes three kids. (The third being my father's daughter, my half-sister, Kerry). The priests at Cathedral of the Holy Cross had been fine with me hanging around the church and even the rectory as long as I was quiet and didn't become a nuisance. But something changed after that day in the attic. My mother was told that I couldn't come to work with her anymore. I could of course come to church for mass on Sunday and the like, and it was okay for me to be there with my ma for a minute if she was just swinging by, but that put an end to my hours wandering around the grounds alone.

TIME AND THE events that followed have, unsurprisingly, transformed my original idea of what happened that day. That indignant priest, while perhaps *acting* like a prick, was not *being* a prick. I see now that his blazing rage contained a great deal of fear, also a kind of anger, which all made sense given how the church had been playing a truly evil game of three-card monte in which priests accused of sexual abuse were moved to Boston, hidden and shuffled, and then, as if this process had somehow rendered them blameless and new, sent to a new parish in another town or even another state. By forbidding me to hang out in the rectory—hell, the whole entire church during off-hours—the angry priest was trying to make sure I didn't become a victim myself.

I'll never know exactly what happened between the angry priest and the kindly one. Did the angry one know or suspect something? Or did the nice priest get punished merely for being too friendly, because in the angry one's mind it was far better for us kids to view priests as hateful assholes and stay far, far away from all of them than to get close and eventually encounter a bad one—or bad ones?

All of this had been happening under the aegis of the charming, broad-faced man that my mother had worked so tirelessly for: Cardinal Law. In 2002, about fifteen years after she'd stopped working at the church, we saw him again, this time on the cover of *Newsweek* magazine. I would also find out that Reverend Raymond P. Messier, the priest for whom I was an altar boy after we moved out of Boston, was accused of multiple accounts of molestation in the seventies and eighties, after which it was promised that he would never work with young boys again. Yet somehow, it was the nineties, and there I was, every Sunday, right next to him as he handed out the sacrament.

More people were coming forward, and *finally*, the sexual abuse that the Catholic Church had covered up and denied, and in the process aided and abetted, was becoming public knowledge. While all these stories were gaining national attention that year, thanks to an investigation by the *Boston Globe*, my parents and I had a hard time talking about it. My mother, so close to everything that had happened yet so in the dark, could barely speak of it at all. As for my father, now a principal at a Catholic high school, he, like my mother, was devastated. After decades of sobriety he had started drinking again, though his time off the wagon wouldn't last long. I remember having a strange, sad, late-night phone conversation with him. He tried to joke with me. "You know what? You should become a priest.

I said, "Why's that?"

"You're a good listener. A decent public speaker. So long as you only slept with consenting adults and kept it to your-self, everyone would love you."

The joke, or whatever odd thing this suggestion of his was, fell flat. I could almost smell the vodka on his breath through the phone. We didn't talk about the scandal again.

By that time, I was nineteen, and I found that everything happening with the Catholic Church seemed far away. Sure, I had those memories of the confessional booth when I was twelve and of all the time I'd spent alone with Reverend Ray (as he liked to be called) where nothing untoward had happened, but which were now marked with my present-day knowledge of who he was, and how the church let him be, and how it was chance or luck or some other factor I can't identify that made it so I did not learn who he was back then. But I had quit attending church in high school. What the Catholic Church did was news, but it didn't matter to me the way it did to my parents.

To my parents, the scandal represented a fundamental, deep, sickeningly multifaceted betrayal. When the institu-tion you've relied on in times of need turns out to be corrupt, who or what can you turn to? Later, after my father quit drinking again and continued to soldier on as a champion for Catholic education, my mother taught second graders at a Catholic school, and together they always attended Mass. Like the Church, with Pope Benedict XVI's retirement and the installation of Pope Francis, my parents would attempt to get their bearings back. But in the early 2000s, similiar to so many other Catholics, they were shaken and scared and felt alone.

Years after, my mother and I finally did talk about it. Just once. We had gotten together in person and were catching up on our weeks. She told me that she and my father had gone to the movies to watch *Spotlight*. I believe it was something that they felt they owed . . . I don't know who. Themselves? The victims? The Church? Was it an effort to remind them *We do not and cannot forget*?

(I wouldn't see *Spotlight* until more than two years later, deciding to watch it in public so I wouldn't become overwhelmed with emotion, which just meant that I ended up full-on sobbing in my front-row, second-story seat on a double-decker Megabus from Boston to New York. No way to suppress or hide my tears so I didn't, catching glimpses of my reflection in the window, my wet face bright and gleaming as I took in the words of Mike Rezendes, journalist on the Spotlight team at the *Boston Globe*, played by Mark Ruffalo: "It could have been you, it could have been me, it could have been any of us." His words hitting my chest.)

When I asked my mother what she thought of the movie, she fell silent. "Did you . . ." she finally said. It seemed to cost her a great effort, to begin asking the question.

"Did you . . ." she said again.

I wouldn't force her to ask the whole question; we both knew what it was. I could see that she'd wondered for a long time. Never really wanting to know the answer.

There were things I could have told her, like the story of the confessional when I was twelve—that a priest had possibly masturbated to my confession or was gathering as many grimy details as possible so he could use them for later, or, to describe it in very general terms, had used his position to use me. I did not feel like telling my mother about this (and definitely did not want to tell her the story I had told in the confessional), and, frankly, I didn't know what that was. I still don't. But I knew one thing for certain, which was that in all my years of being involved with the Catholic Church, as a young kid hanging out at the Cathedral of the Holy Cross and as a slightly older one serving as altar boy with Reverend Ray, nobody had ever touched me.

I'd never been molested.

So I rushed to answer her, to set her heart at ease.

"No, ma. Never." I watched as her shoulders loosened, then pulled her close for a hug.

I was grateful to be able to tell her the truth. I was grateful to know that she no longer had to wonder, was no longer stuck between wanting to know and worrying that to ask me would break open unimaginable reservoirs of pain in myself and our family. I was grateful that I could tell she'd cared about the answer long before she could bring herself to ask. Of course she had.

In that moment I understood more deeply than ever before why the victims didn't come forward sooner. There are all kinds of reasons, of course—the Church, and the world, do so much to punish victims who tell the truth.

But also, if my truth had been different, and I had shared it with her, I would have broken her heart utterly and completely. In no way, shape, or form would it have been my fault, but that is what would have resulted. Which is yet another pernicious aspect of the Church's cover-up of sexual abuse: They wanted the problem to go away and add up to nothing, and therefore made every part of the equation nothing—nobody knowing, because the truth would be too horrifying to accept, too horrifying to even share, and, thus, nobody having to be punished. To cover up their crimes was to scrub the fault off the perpetrators, because if nothing happened, nobody was at fault, and who would believe such terrible acts from men of God?

But they did happen, so the fault would still have existed, only now floating free and waiting for a bearer. And if my answer to my mother's question had been yes, it would have cleaved her heart right down the center and that fault would have settled heavy upon my shoulders. The kind of fault that never, ever, ever, ever should fall to a victim, wherein the Church's denial of their reality forces the victims to fight to tell the truth that *nothing* was actually *something*. It forces the victims to be the ones to make it real.

And if they don't? How many victims out there wanted desperately for nothing to have happened to them, and thus would say nothing? Given the alternatives—the fault on my shoulders, my mother's shattered heart—I think I might have taken that secret to my grave. The Church knew it, too; institutional leaders like Cardinal Law used that knowledge and bet on it. To this day, I say I didn't know what happened in that confessional when I was twelve. And I don't. But I have always been ashamed to bring it up with my family. With my friends. I'd play it down and pretend it was nothing. But one could argue that a priest jerking off two feet away from me, having me recite lurid details of a sexual experience so he could live vicariously through me—me, who had been a *child*—was *something*. I still have a problem saying that. Because to acknowledge it was something is to admit that something happened *to* me.

But in that moment with my mother I said nothing.

I pulled out of the hug and asked her a question I had avoided asking her for years.

"Did you know?" I said.

She didn't answer right away. I wondered if other people in her life had asked her this before.

"No, Isaac," she said. "That's what went wrong. None of us knew. So many of them knew, and so many of us didn't. Until it was far too late."

DITCHING CATHOLICISM DIDN'T make me any less Catholic. Plenty of lapsed Catholics out there know exactly what I mean. I'd been edging away from Catholicism gradually, until suddenly my whole life changed at age fourteen and there was no more room for it.

Desperate to get out of my house—and maybe a subconscious part of me I'd never have admitted to at the time agreed with my folks that I was on a bad path—I had applied for and gotten a full scholarship to a boarding school. I had no idea what came next, but I knew it meant leaving home. I was grateful.

The first Sunday at boarding school I woke up like I was already late for something. It didn't dawn on me until that exact moment that . . . I no longer had to go to church. That first Sunday felt magical. As if I and I alone had been gifted extra time in a day. Church was only an hour, but its absence transformed my weekends.

From then on, I was never again a practicing Catholic. I don't regret it, though occasionally there are things I miss about church. The high, exalted feeling of my soul full to the brim after Sunday Mass (though I only truly felt this when I was a kid and suspect that even if I were a practicing Catholic now this joy would be lost to me). The fun of getting together with a large group of people and belting out songs. Like some sort of religious group karaoke. A very pious kind of karaoke, sure, but karaoke nonetheless. Plus, there's wine.

Most importantly, I can't deny that there's something pretty great about making a dedicated space—just one hour a week out of your life—to express gratitude for what the universe has given you, to apologize for the ways in which you have wronged yourself and others, and to be present and around people, both familiar and strangers alike. My time in that space has shaped my entire life.

I am grateful for everything, including the sanctity of my body and my very existence. As an adult, I don't believe in God, but I still pray anytime I'm in trouble, or feeling lost, or alone, which is to say I still do it almost daily.

I try to be kind to others, and when I fall short, which is often, I blame myself and vow to do better. I also try to forgive myself. We're all sinners, after all. That's another thing the Church taught me. We're all sinners, and that's just the way it is, and that's okay. Although I'm grateful to the epic, fantastic, nutty stories of the Bible for being mental TV for me when I had no real TV growing up, I prefer to set aside my memories of the fire and brimstone and fear and shame and punishment and hold on to the blessing of forgiveness, both of others and oneself. Up until a point.

In one way, the Catholic Church's sexual abuse scandal could be seen as the dictum "Forgiveness above all else" being taken to an opportunistic, self-serving, evil extreme. And anyway, that is not real forgiveness. Real forgiveness requires taking responsibility, because real forgiveness is not complete in and of itself—it's a first step. You forgive first to acknowledge your own or another's wrongdoing, then to make a kind of peace with it—to lay it to rest because the past can't be changed—and finally to move forward *better*. An institution meant to be a beacon of hope for people, often in poor and marginalized communities whose place in the power structures of the Church and society at large made them especially vulnerable, should have known all this. It is the greatest betrayal and hypocrisy that they chose to ignore it.

TO BE VERY blasphemously honest, I consider my most real and tangible vestiges of Catholicism to be my tattoos.

One of my favorite sayings is "Life mistakes are my copilot." My tattoos are a collection of either mistakes themselves or are my way of recording some of my most important mistakes.

More than half of them are actually rooted in Catholic lore—the most overt and straightforward example being my large tattoo of Saint Jude, with his staff and medallion of Jesus, imprinted on my right arm with the caption "Lost Cause."

Growing up, when I was still a child of faith, my favorite book was a slim volume called *The Children's Book of Saints* by Louis M. Savary. Each page bore an illustration of a saint— Saint Francis of Assisi, Saint Agnes, Saint Thomas Aquinas, around fifty in all—along with brief biographical information and stories. Underneath each illustration was a prayer to the saint, as well as each saint's feast date. I would read the book in my bedroom in our small apartment, whispering prayers and doing my best to memorize those feast days.

I don't remember if Saint Jude was included in the book, but he is the patron saint of desperate cases and lost causes (as well as a few football clubs in Brazil and Europe). My mother gave me my first Saint Jude medal when I was twelve, which could have felt like calling it a little early. But in her defense, I had already gotten into a lot of trouble as a twelve-year-old, and her point (and her hope) was unmistakable to me. Since then, I've worn a Saint Jude medal most of my life, losing one and replacing it and losing that one too.

A while ago, after I'd lost my umpteenth medal, I decided I'd do the sensible thing and make it official by getting Saint Jude tattooed on me. I loved him, the idea of him—as a sometimes lost cause myself throughout my life—because I loved rooting for the underdog and witnessing the miracles that can bloom out of low expectations. The miracle of even *trying* when failure and ignominy haunt your steps.

Most of all? I love the *reason* Saint Jude is the patron saint of lost causes. Jude basically needed good posthumous PR and the Catholic Church gave it to him. Why the need for good PR? People wouldn't pray to Saint Jude because they were worried God would think they were praying to Judas Iscariot, Christ's snitch. So the church was like, "Hey, everyone, Jude here is so desperate for prayers that he'll help you out no matter how shitty the situation you're in."

And there you have it: Saint Jude got to be the patron saint of lost causes by being thirsty. My dude *needs* prayers and will help you out, no matter how fucked the situation is, because homie is desperate too. As an inveterate people pleaser, let's just say I relate to this.

Finally, that staff (or sometimes club or spear or axe) Saint Jude is often portrayed with? That's actually the weapon he was killed with when he was martyred. Which is to say this: Saint Jude's not only the president of desperate cases and lost causes. He's also a client!

Catholicism wasn't for me, but it's in me; it's around me; it's a lens I look through sometimes without even consciously realizing it. It's in and on my skin. In so many ways, I can't help but carry the Catholic Church and its philosophies with me, always, even though I left the church long ago.

GLASTONBURY ABBEY IN Hingham, Massachusetts, has a majestic chapel. Where the Cathedral of the Holy Cross is large and looming and stone, the Glastonbury Abbey's new chapel, built in 2001, is modest and wooden, all the better to blend in with the surrounding rolling green fields and tall pines that reach far above the steeple. The prior of the abbey is Brother Daniel, who lived at John Leary House in a single-room occupancy and worked with the Catholic Worker when my family lived in Boston. On the Abbey's website there is a whole section about the "Protection of Children and Vulnerable Adults."

My half-sister, Kerry, lives in Hingham, a wealthy suburb of Boston, in a large house by the water with her husband and their son. She didn't have it easy growing up but has done well for herself, and hosts Christmas for the whole family every year. My brother, Joel, hosts a similar gathering on Thanksgiving. Essentially, both of my siblings have realized what an awesome power it is to give birth to a new generation. It is like being able to sound an ancient magical horn, and when the rest of the family hears the call, we are helpless to resist; we must come from wherever we are scattered and piece ourselves back into one clan. Long-divorced grandparents all coming together, talking to one another, getting along, all in the name of the li'l ones. I'm glad of it.

This past Christmas we went to Glastonbury Abbey for Christmas Mass. Sunlight pierced the chapel, not through stained glass but through triangular windows subdivided into smaller triangles and diamonds. I didn't miss all the colors and opulence, not when confronted with the beauty of simplicity and clarity.

The pulpit and altar were in the center, instead of at the front of the chapel, so the priest gave his sermon surrounded by brothers and congregants. The Mass was moving, and while it didn't fill my soul in the way that the Masses of my childhood did, I found myself experiencing the calm that I'm sure is part of why my parents keep coming back again and again.

As I exited the church, two older women at the door wished me a Merry Christmas, and then, when they noticed all my tattoos, both gave me a smile that was as sweet as it was pitying and disappointed and proceeded to give me half a dozen of the most patronizing pats I've ever received. For a brief moment I considered pointing out my Saint Jude and other Catholic-themed tattoos, but I feared this would only encourage more pats.

In the parking lot, Brother Daniel, despite the fact that we hadn't seen each other in almost thirty years, came over and gave me a hug. We talked. It was soothing to catch up. We talked about the Benedictines (my father had gone on retreats to a Benedictine monastery out in North Central Massachusetts, one of the reasons I believe we ended up there) and

Saint Benedict, who *was* in *The Children's Book of Saints*, and had started an order that was centered on community, hours of silence, and a dedication to prayer and work. Unlike so much of the Catholic Church, it is the opposite of opulent. The Benedictines have no hierarchy other than designating an abbot of the monastery, and even the monasteries are each independent and autonomous. As I get older, the simplicity of the Benedictines, and their closeness to nature (much like that of Saint Francis), speaks to me in the same way I'm sure it first spoke to my father.

As I said, my parents are still very much Catholic. Following the scandal, they grieved; they returned; they devoted a lot of their lives to Catholic education. The older I get, and the greater my distance from organized religion grows, the easier it is for me to see what Catholicism has meant to them.

My father is always quick to remind me of the charity performed by the Catholic Church, and I know in his heart he wishes the Vatican just . . . wasn't there, so that the money in its coffers could be spread among the poor of the world. He wishes that the teachings of Jesus (with a side of Thomas Merton and Dorothy Day) were more strictly followed. My parents, whether they'd care to say it or not, are socialists. As is the Catholic Worker. In a way, my parents love the faith, but hate the institution. Which of course becomes dicey when ideals meet the real world, and the institution is the one with all the money who pays your bills.

Both of my parents were at a low point in their lives when they joined the Catholic Worker, both as human beings without a home who benefited from the organization's generosity, and as members of the organization themselves who believed there was beauty to be found in poverty and in a faith based on forgiveness for past sins. Catholicism gave my parents hope and focus and direction and community. It helped them when they had nothing, then helped them to improve their material standing in the world. I hope my parents know that, despite everything else, I have always been proud of how they practice their faith even as I decided it wasn't for me, and I'm proud of their calling as educators.

My parents and I will never find a common ground in the Church. They taught me too well: Love the faith. Hate the institution. My faith is my own, but I learned it from them. When I was a child my father and I would go camping at the place where he had brought my mother early in their relationship, living for days or even weeks in the woods. The woods is where I was conceived. A closeness to nature, for me, is a closeness to God. That is about as spiritual as I can get these days, and it is enough.

I'll never attend church regularly again. I'll never sit for confession again. But I can't deny that on Christmas morning, in the right church, with the right people, the sunlight cutting across the crucifixion can be a beautiful thing. Speaking and singing old, old phrases together can be a beautiful thing. Still, the best part of visiting Glastonbury Abbey is walking among the nearby pines. I believe that has always been true for my mother and father too. That despite the endless ways in which we diverge, we agree on this: There is always a place to talk to God, even if it's a God you don't believe in.

Confessions of a Former Former Fat Kid

The slap of my mother's hand against my bare stomach rings out and fills the entire store.

I watch as my belly jiggles in the floor-to-ceiling mirror mounted on the column in front of us. We're surrounded by racks of cheap clothes in terrible colors. In the mirror, my mother looks me right in the eyes, her other hand pinning my shirt up to expose my midriff. "If you weren't getting so fat, I wouldn't have to buy you new clothes," she says. My skin stings as the red mark of her hand fades. I pull my shirt back down and refuse to cry.

We're at a Stuarts in Athol, Massachusetts. Stuarts was like Walmart for poor communities in New England back before Walmart realized it should be Walmart for poor communities in New England (and everywhere else). I am eight years old. Growing. Getting bigger.

When we lived in Boston, my father made sure that I got exercise, taking me out for long bike rides while he ran alongside me. But Dad stayed in Boston and Ma and I moved out to the country. "You'll have a yard," Ma said, and I pretended to be happy. I tried to play in the yard, but it didn't make up for the lack of bike rides. Or the Chef Boyardee for dinner most nights, or the pasta and butter with a side of bread on the others. Ma had been bigger, too, when she was younger, and she wanted so badly to save me from the same fate. It didn't help that now we were living next to her parents in rural Massachusetts, in a town she'd promised herself she would escape, a town she *had* successfully escaped right up until she hadn't.

Now we lived in the house next to her parents in the town where she had been a big girl. Now my mom lived with her son but without her husband, who had to stay in the city because "there aren't enough jobs out here," which I found strange because there seemed to be plenty of jobs for my friends' dads, and "not enough jobs" didn't explain why Ma cried most nights and why her ma, my grandma, looked at me like I was the garbage someone forgot to take out. I'd sneak bowls of cereal when no one was home, pouring sugar and honey on the off-brand Cheerios pretending they were the Honey Nut kind, the kind my other grandma—who lived near the ocean and never looked at me like I was trash— always fed me. I would wash the bowl before Ma got home from work. She would cry and I would hug her and do the only thing I knew how to do, which was not cry.

The same way I don't cry now, under the fluorescent lights at Stuarts, surrounded by clothes that don't fit and we can't afford.

IT'S SUMMER. I'M sixteen years old and I'm the skinniest I've ever been thanks to a diet of running, cigarettes, and snorted Ritalin (usually) and Adderall (when I can get my hands on it). Most days I drive my mother's three-colored car (all different shades of blue) to Gardner, Massachusetts, the closest town with any downtown to speak of, where I have a job at a Friendly's washing dishes.

At the beginning of the summer, the weight seemed to fall off me. But right up until that moment I'd been all the terrible euphemisms that were so much worse than simply being called fat: "husky," "chunky," "portly," "big-boned," "plump." Words ingrained into the fabric of my being. They were a part of me, which is probably why, when the weight disappeared, I didn't even notice that it was gone.

I kept to myself at Friendly's. I listened to bad rap as I scraped ice cream out of sticky glass containers, the industrial washer making the air wet, my bleached-blond hair sticking to my forehead. When I dragged giant garbage bags of half-eaten hamburgers to the large metal bins behind the building, I'd take breaks to smoke damp Newports alone.

Most of the waitresses were older than my mother, and would sneak food home to their kids and husbands, but a few of them were my age, working for the summer. They'd smile at me in ways that no girls had before. I couldn't for the life of me understand why.

One day, a young waitress comes up to me and says, "I'm having a party." Her name tag reads JENNIFER and she is the prettiest human to talk to me in months.

"What's that?" I say, removing my headphones, Eminem mixing with the clanging of the dishwasher.

"I said I'm having a party and you should come. You know, a house party."

It's one of those moments so improbable that I must be imagining it—but also so wonderful, so hoped for and delicious and exactly like the kind of nineties teen movie I never thought I'd get to be in, except maybe as a chubby extra, that I desperately want it to be real.

I'd never been invited to a party by a girl before. Though I'd been drinking and doing drugs since I was twelve, to me parties meant slamming beers alone in the woods, or slamming beers with my friends in the woods until we became brave or stupid enough to fight each other. We'd pair off, throwing fists into each other's faces until blood burst from our noses, lips, and once, only once, this guy Mike's eye. My friends, all skinny, always with their shirts off even before the fighting started. Me always with my shirt firmly on, keeping covered, trying to wash the bloodstains out the next day.

Jennifer scribbles on her order pad and hands me her address. "Bring something fun," she says, and walks away.

That summer, I'll lose my virginity.

"WAY TO NOT be so fat, Fitzgerald!" Hunter yells as I pass him in the hallway at boarding school. A varsity hockey player, Hunter was infamous for hooking up with all of the most attractive girls at school. He liked telling racist jokes and prided himself on his bluntness. His favorite phrase was "Lighten up, man."

Despite the triumphs of the previous summer, plus everyone at school weirdly telling me how "nice" I looked when we returned in the fall, it isn't until this moment—as an actual character in that nineties teen movie, albeit one getting yelled at by a jock—that I realize I've lost weight.

It's also when I realize that my weight and how I perceive myself aren't at all related. I still *feel* fat. Ugly. Unattractive. Every time I look in the mirror I can still see my mother's red handprint fading to white as my belly shakes.

Hunter's words ring in my ears, a confusing mix of pride and shame taking hold. "Not be so fat" means I still am fat, that I used to be more so. It means fat is bad and getting skinnier is good, no matter how I actually feel about myself.

We learn so many lessons in high school, most of them terrible. I carry Hunter's words in my head like a medal or a trophy. One that burns me as I hold it, even as I refuse to put it down.

THE OTHER LESSON I quickly learn is that no matter how I feel about my body, I feel better about it while having sex. Or at least I can forget about it—its weight, its size, its bulk—for a little while, the same way I can temporarily forget about gravity every time I ride a skateboard. If I don't like the way my body looks, I can at least trick other people into liking it. And that's how it felt: like a trick. A sleight of hand. A way to fool someone into desiring me, if only for a short time, even if I was undesirable to myself. And I became quite good at it.

After losing my virginity the summer I was sixteen, I quickly found someone else who would sleep with me, and then another. It was harder when I was back in school, at least initially, surrounded by lacrosse players and basketball stars, boys quick to pop their tops off at the drop of a hat, while I kept my T-shirt on even at the beach.

But then I started running even more and adding dip to my all-cigarette diet while upping my nose's intake of my friends' prescription amphetamines. I still hated my body, but by high school societal standards (you know, basically like regular societal standards but with a scoop of youthful cruelty to give it that zing) I was moving in the right direction. I became more popular, and by the time senior year rolled around I found myself getting laid during the school year almost as much as during the summer.

The habit of letting attention from other people stand in for liking myself continued into college and after, when I moved to San Francisco. Sex not because the person and I liked each other a whole lot (although sometimes we did) or even sex just for sex's sake, but sex because I wanted the person to like me, or at least tolerate me, ever so briefly.

Woe is me, right? I'd be lying if I said it wasn't *fun as hell* to be young and free and jumping into bed with people. It was! But through the high of seeing myself reflected in someone else's eyes as an attractive person, a guy worth having sex with, I was ignoring how much I needed other people to like me. The good times were spackle over my body-image issues—sexy, fun spackle, but spackle nonetheless.

And after sex, no matter if we were at their place or mine, no matter if it was an attempt to start a relationship or (much more likely) a one-night stand, I would always put my shirt on first. Immediately. I would slip from the covers and grab my shirt from the floor and slip it over my head, the post-sex rush of anxiety and self-loathing quieting only after I had covered my torso.

As my number of partners climbed, my confidence in myself stayed the same. Flat. Empty. Not that I wasn't good at faking it. "I'm an FFK," I'd say.

"An FFK?"

"A former fat kid." And I'd wait for laughter.

RECENTLY, MY FRIEND Mikael Kennedy—once a vaga-bond, now a successful photographer—emailed me a picture he took of me when I was twenty-three, from those early San Francisco days. Mikael had been eating Dexedrine and driving around the United States for weeks with another buddy whose name escapes me. I remember I stole them some food from the restaurant I was working at, and then we went to spend what little money we had on beer. We drank in the street. I don't know how Mikael got me to take my shirt off but I do remember that I was bleeding. "Isaac," he said, and I looked up.

I look at this picture and wince, because I can see now—*now* I can see—what I looked like. I keenly see the difference between what the picture shows and what my own memories hold. Mikael's photo displays a jawline, a rib cage (too much of one). A negative space where the body that's been

haunting me my whole life should be. I keep looking for it, and find nothing.

When it comes to body-image issues, we are all in our own personal hells. And my hell is but a flickering Bic lighter when compared with others. But that's the thing about hells: Comparing them does not lead you to the exit door of your own. Even as I grew older, matured, found somewhat more stable relationships, even as my weight fluctuated, my sense of self never did. Not once did I like what I saw in the mirror whenever I saw myself in it.

When I moved to New York City at the age of thirty, the harsh East Coast winters crashed into my slowing metabolism. It didn't help that I had stopped smoking cigarettes (soon after), doing dip (long before), and putting study drugs up my nose (thank god). I gained forty pounds.

As I write this in my late thirties, my weight continues to fluctuate. At this point, I know there will be no moment of revelation. There will be no ideal weight where I'll look at myself and say, "Yes. This." Instead of looking for a perfect body, which I have done my entire life, I understand I will never be perfect. I'm learning to be okay with that.

That's my own personal exit. An exit I haven't yet walked through but one I try to approach instead of back away from, every day.

Which is to say, of course, that sometimes I am still dissatisfied with my body—there are mornings the pants don't zip up without a fight, and growing older sure ain't helping. But I don't spend nearly as much time hating myself as I did when I was younger. I don't fall headlong into that pit; I just can't, or won't. I've wasted way too much youth on self-hatred as it is.

It's been thirty years since I was eight years old in a Stuarts in Massachusetts, and twenty-two years since I realized I don't truly see myself when I look into a mirror. But now I no longer grab a T-shirt directly after sex, and when I do see my own reflection, I work hard to not loathe what I see. To see a person, rather than an assemblage of shit that needs to be fixed. I try to be okay with that person, even when—just sometimes—I glimpse the imprint of a hand, fading from red to white.

The True Story of My Teenage Fight Club

We weren't new to violence. Our families were scattered; our community was rural and poor. Violence was the solution, problem, and consequence. It was Nate Murphy slamming you into the shit-green lockers as you walked down the hallway minding your own business, or your father exploding into the shower to smack you because you took the Lord's name in vain while getting ready for school. Sometimes it was quieter: coming home to find your mother sitting slumped at the bottom of the basement stairs with a pill bottle still in her hand, the empty fifth of vodka rolling on the concrete floor, somehow unbroken.

We were used to all those kinds of violence. But we were new to the kind that was controlled, contained. We'd never encountered anything like this.

"I want you to hit me as hard as you can," said the man in the movie.

After our first time watching *Fight Club*, me and my buddy Sean didn't even speak. We just hung out in the bathroom, then snuck right back into the theater. Soon all the rest of my friends had seen it, too. It was 1999 and we were fifteen and sixteen, bumming rides from each other or older kids down from the hills to the Hampshire Mall or over to Leominster. We were the right age, the right amount of troubled, and, most of all, the right amount of stupid for this movie. Just when we were ready for *Fight Club*, we got it.

Fight Club, which was David Fincher's adaptation of a 1996 novel by Chuck Palahniuk, is a certain kind of teen boy's dream. The unnamed narrator (Edward Norton) is a bored man who meets another man named Tyler Durden (Brad Pitt), his vibrant opposite and a Manic Pixie Dream Bro for the ages. Durden becomes the narrator's cool best friend and teaches him how to interact with (i.e., punch) other men through the titular fight club. They also fight over a woman named Marla Singer (Helena Bonham Carter) who is weird and reckless and hot, although the true romance of the film is really between the two men. Then (surprise!) we find out that they are actually the *same* man, proving that Ed Norton had the power inside him to be cool all along. Now, instead of friendship he has respect and power. Looked up to as a leader by men all across the land, he successfully brings down the credit card industry, reverting all debt to $0, and wins the girl (who seems fine with how crazy and destructive he's been, because plot device).

For me and my friends, the movie had everything: sex, death, nihilism, friendship, a warped view of love. The central tenet of *Fight Club* was *not* talking about stuff, which is very important to boys who like to pretend they don't have feelings. It looked cool, and the people in it were cool in the exact ways each one of us wanted to be cool. It broke the fourth wall, even though, rubes that we were, we barely had a clue that the fourth wall existed. And prior to *Fight Club*, had any of us known about this amazing band called the Pixies? We had not.

Most of all, the movie espoused a heroically half-baked Nietzschean philosophy about destroying society just for the fuck of it that resonated, because we, like so many young men do, felt unimportant and powerless. "The things you own end up owning you," the movie told us, which we loved because we didn't own shit.

We already knew we were not special, but *Fight Club* transformed our very lack of specialness into something special. "Listen up, maggots," Durden says into a literal megaphone in the movie. "You are not special. You are not a beautiful or unique snowflake. You're the same decaying organic matter as everything else." When you're young, these things affect you. When you're poor, even more so.

"You are not your job. You're not how much money you have in the bank. You are not the car you drive. You're not the contents of your wallet. You're not your fucking khakis. You are the all-singing, all-dancing crap of the world."

Only a few of us had cars, and none of us had money, but it didn't matter. *Fight Club* told us that what we did have—our bodies, our anger, our clear-eyed belief that so much of the world was shit and farcical and irrelevant—was all that we needed.

I DON'T REMEMBER whose idea it was to start our own fight club. All I know is we tried it for the first time at Connor's house, where we did everything worth doing.

Connor's house was like all our houses, but worse. We lived in the middle of nowhere, but Connor's house was straight-up in the woods. Our homes were heated with wood stoves and riddled with holes, which bugs crawled through, but Connor's had only just gotten running water. He basically lived in a treehouse from an Ewok village—if you squinted your eyes and ignored the cars rotting in the front yard.

My friendship with Connor was one of those friendships you know is going to be special from the moment you meet the other person, even if the actual specialness doesn't come right away. For a while, it's just both of you standing around waiting to be the true friends you're meant to be, until there's that moment of connection that changes everything. In our case we were in seventh grade, hating life, trying to get through a shitty school field trip at a museum, when we somehow ended up bonding over our fathers. Mine was absent and angry, his dead. From then on, more or less, we were best friends.

A lot of us had parents who were never around, but Connor's mom was better than absent: She just didn't care, in the best way possible. She'd come right home from her part-time job, have a few drinks, and go to bed early. Her brand of not caring felt like a blessing; she really, truly did love us, and we understood each other, and she left us the hell alone.

It's strange to call Connor's house a safe place, given all the dumb and dangerous shit we did there, but it was—a house where nothing was chasing us, where the only trouble was the trouble we made ourselves. There was always food in the fridge and DVDs to watch, and you never got hit in the bad way, the unfair way, where it was just adults unleashing their frustration on you. But that doesn't mean we didn't hit each other.

We liked hurting ourselves. In middle school Connor and I fought no-holds-barred BB gun battles, our heads filled with *Platoon* and *Full Metal Jacket* and *Apocalypse Now*. We painted our faces with mud and loaded up our army surplus store backpacks with bottle rockets and Roman candles and anything that could be set on fire. One evening, when it was raining too hard, we brought the fight inside. Pinned down by heavy fire from Connor, I was stuck hiding in the bathtub until I came up with a brilliant new weapon: a homemade flamethrower composed of my cigarette lighter and his mom's Aqua Net. The bathroom wall caught fire, and we had to douse the blaze with water from the toilet.

The war games quickly gave way to *Jackass*-style stupidity: throwing ourselves into ravines, riding a busted baby carriage down the hill behind the house, hotboxing the junked cars in Connor's front yard, and jumping off his raised-on-stilts front porch "just because." We were teenage terrors and we were profoundly bored, both qualities compounding each other.

The leap from shooting each other with BB guns to punching each other in the face was not a big one. It started with one-hits; we'd square up against each other and go blow for blow. First one to fall or call it quits lost. But more often than not, it would break out into an actual fight, so eventually we just said, "Fuck it, let's do it like they did it in *Fight Club*." Usually we didn't plan in advance—there were no cell phones, no email. Boys just showed up at Connor's house like it was a teenage dirtbag Neverland.

So many of these fights blur together, but I'll never forget my first. It was with one of the Mikes. There were a lot of guys named Mike; this particular Mike was funny and kind, liked to climb trees shirtless while yelling at the sky, high and drunk and pulling down wood for our bonfires with his bare hands. In the house upstairs, Connor's mother was asleep. There weren't many people over. With a few beers in each of us, we stood shoulder to shoulder in the kitchen, of all places.

Mike swung first. His fist hit my mouth and my first thought was "Fuck, no way my folks can afford the dentist." No way we could replace my already fake tooth from when it had been knocked out in the fourth grade during a real fight over a basketball. My head snapped back, and then came right up as my fists started flailing. I was more stunned than in pain; the pain came later. As we fought, my fists bounced against Mike's hard, sinewy body while his seemed to sink into my heavier frame. For a moment I had him up against the fridge, and our boys let out the "OHHHHHH" that always felt so good to hear. Then his fist landed on the bridge of my nose and stars exploded into my vision. After that, Mike must have swept my leg or just pushed me over, because suddenly I was looking up at the ceiling of Connor's kitchen, yellow with cigarette smoke, and Mike was offering to help me up.

"Want to go again?" he said.

When there got to be too many of us, we started fighting in the quarry down the dirt road. We looked beat up a lot of the time, but what was the difference? Teachers didn't take much notice, and we wanted to treat our wounds casually, just like the movie did. None of us were really popular or unpopular in high school. Some of us did more drugs than others, and some of us played football while others got drunk underneath the bleachers, but for the most part we got along because we didn't have shit-all else to do.

Watching was almost as much fun as fighting. We'd make a circle around the fighters, shouting encouragement. The mood was bloodthirsty and cheerful; usually we were rooting for both of them. No winners or losers, just the guy who stayed up and the guy who went down.

As in the movie, most of the guys fought with their shirts off, pants slung low. I always kept mine on. My friends knew that they were something to be looked at; they were performing when they shucked their tacky Hawaiian shirts and stood there dressed only in baggy cargo pants. (Another nice thing about *Fight Club*: Its thrift-store style was *highly* attainable, and boy did we take advantage.)

We pretended; we postured so hard, wearing aviators we'd stolen from gas stations. But, you know, our fight club *did work*. We did get closer to and were more supportive of each other. That was real. Who knows if it was the way the actual fighting affected us or the way the movie told us we would become closer, but it happened. Connor was kind of the leader; he wasn't the loudest and bossiest, rather, he was the most caring and thoughtful among us. Maybe it was because he had a little brother or because he knew he had a responsibility to us since it was his tumbledown house, presided over by his loving, negligent mother, that sheltered us all. It was perfect for those of us who didn't live there, but maybe hard on an eldest son.

The last time we fought was in Connor's living room, where one of the Mikes knocked another Mike so hard that a blood vessel in his eye burst. Immediately the white part of his eye went red, and against it his iris gleamed a shocking blue, and it was horrible and beautiful and like nothing we'd ever seen before. Eyes had been blackened and noses bloodied, but nothing like this. Someone said, "Has his pupil been knocked loose? I heard you can go blind from that." We took one of the frozen burritos from Connor's fridge and held it to his face.

THERE WAS NO big discussion; we just stopped fighting after that. More of us got our driver's licenses and girls started to show up at our parties and the only reason anyone punched anyone was because of them, because we thought they cared. They did not.

After we stopped, we heard rumors that other folks were still doing it. "Murphy's got the key to the Rod and Gun Club by his house, and he's hosting fights in the basement." "Two towns over they've got one going in the parking lot behind the Star Market."

I never knew if any of the stories were true, but we all wanted to believe them because it made life feel that much more like the movie. It felt good to think that we were the people to have started it, as if we were the only juvenile delinquents in the whole world who had seen this movie and decided that fighting each other would be a good idea.

We all graduated in 2001. I'd gone to a different high school for years, thanks to a scholarship, and Connor cleaned up his act, too, at least a little bit, graduating at the top of his class. He helped out on yearbook, and one of his duties was to create a flyer to be passed out to all of the students and teachers and families at graduation. He filled it with unattributed inspirational quotes, some of which were also in the yearbook itself. Every last one of those quotes came from *Fight Club*. At one point in the movie, Brad Pitt tells Edward Norton, "It's only after we've lost everything that we're free to do anything." I'm pretty sure that ended up being the class motto. Most of the Mikes went into the armed services. So did Connor. He leads troops now, surrounded by young, violent men. He does his best to care for them, just as he did for us.

But that wouldn't be until years later. In 1999, we still hadn't outgrown our yearning for the end of the world. On New Year's Eve, at the very end of 1999, we were rooting for Y2K. The snow was heavy that year and Connor, his little brother, and I sat in their dilapidated house, feeding wood into his stove, passing the time talking about what we'd do if the power grids went down. Who wouldn't want a restart? We'd go out and help the elderly and get everyone to a central location with a generator. We'd rebuild society (but not too much of it) with a focus on community and agriculture and also definitely lower the drinking age and make cigarettes free.

We still fought. Connor's little brother threw my cigarettes in the fire because he said he didn't want me to die, and so I beat him up. Not in the *Fight Club* way, but in that old way, the violence in me uncontained. When I was done I felt calm again. I stole a pack of GPCs from Connor's mom and tried to console his brother. My anger was the anger of a young man, which flares ferociously and then is wiped clean, like it never existed in the first place. Connor's brother wouldn't talk to me except to whisper, "Fuck you."

"Think it'll all be over?" Connor had said, almost hopefully. But by the time I'd beaten up his little brother, the New Year had swept around the world and there had been no radical shift in society. We watched the ball drop in some city we'd never been to. Afterward, the programming came back to the local channel, which was based miles and miles from where we lived. We watched as a young reporter came on screen to test her ATM card. "Let's see if Y2K has struck," she said chirpily.

Connor and I leaned forward in our seats as she put her card in, covered the keypad, and typed in her code, smiling at the camera as it zoomed in on the ATM screen. The screen flashed red. Card declined.

Connor and I stared at each other. His brother even looked at us, the beating temporarily forgiven.

"Holy shit!"

For three brief thirty-second commercial spots we felt like it had happened. We were getting our restart, just like Tyler Durden predicted:

> In the world I see, you are stalking elk through the damp canyon forests around the ruins of Rockefeller Center. You'll wear leather clothes that will last you the rest of your life. You'll climb the wrist-thick kudzu vines that wrap the Sears Tower. And when you look down, you'll see tiny figures pounding corn, laying strips of venison on the empty carpool lane of some abandoned superhighway.

It was really happening.

"Whoops!" said the reporter, embarrassed, when the news came back on. "Sorry about that. Seems I had overdrawn my account." She reassured the viewing audience that there had been a mistake and Y2K was bubkes and everything was still online, which we really should have figured out on our own, considering that she was still in front of us on the TV.

The world hadn't gotten its movie ending, so there would be nothing to draw people together who did not want to be together. Gone dads would stay gone, slightly less poor kids would mock poorer kids, bad would not hit rock bottom but rather keep getting worse. There was no end to it. The year 2000 had arrived, with all of the constraints and conditions of every previous year we had seen, and the world's trajectory as we knew it would not stop, no matter how badly we wanted it to.

Dirtbag, Massachusetts

In eighth grade I hit Dave Stoll in the face with my math book because he called me "tubby." Like it was my name. "Hey, Tubby."

But really, I hit Dave Stoll in the face with a math book because I was mad. Mad at the insult, sure. But I was also mad at my parents and mad at my home life and mad at the world. A friend, Chad, had died earlier that year. A rare heart condition. That didn't seem right nor fair. So little in life did.

But also, Dave had called me "tubby."

So I hit Dave Stoll in the face with my math book and watched as his body spun around and his face bounced off the locker behind him.

"You're lucky you didn't break his nose," the assistant principal said later, as I sat in his office and stared out the window.

I may not have broken Dave Stoll's nose, but it sure bled like I had.

WHEN PEOPLE ASKED me how I got into boarding school, my answer was usually, "I hit Dave Stoll in the face with my math book," which wasn't entirely true. But wasn't untrue either.

My home life was fucked, but my grades were good and my standardized test scores were better. After the math book incident I was suspended for a week, but because my school couldn't guarantee I'd be supervised at home (which was true of most students in my town), I had to have an in-school suspension. Every morning I'd quickly finish the work I was given, and by the second day I was spending my extra time helping out the school librarian or the school secretaries with their work.

The librarian and the secretaries took notice. One of them was Chad's mother. She already cared about me as one of her son's close friends, and maybe wanted to help me realize that fucking up my life was pointless, even cruelly so, when kids like Chad never even got a chance to fuck up theirs.

There was a school she knew of. A boarding school. They sometimes offered scholarships to local kids. Especially those who might be in trouble but showed "promise." Whatever that meant. It might be a good option for me. The librarians would help me fill out the forms to apply.

It was hard for me to accept help when offered—it still is. But they waited, kept offering. Until finally I had to admit it was what I wanted.

THE TOWN WHERE I grew up had the highest teenage pregnancy rate per capita in the state of Massachusetts. Later in life, while doing research, I came across this line describing the area: "Geographically isolated from the major cultural centers of Massachusetts; consequently its residents tend to create their own entertainment." Followed almost immediately by "many publicized social problems . . . Chief among [them] are high rates of unemployment, teenage pregnancy, domestic violence, and alcoholism."

There was nothing to do in these old mill towns but fuck, get fucked up, or fuck somebody else up. We spent our days doing drugs, driving around in trucks, drinking beer, and listening to music. Some of us had more money than others, but nobody had much of it. We were poor kids in a poor area of a rich state. Everybody's families had their issues, but even by regional standards my friends knew something was off in my home. Some of their parents realized it too. They'd feed me, let me stay the night.

But it wasn't until I hit Dave Stoll in the face with a math book that teachers began to take notice. Or, okay, maybe it wasn't just the math book but also the other bad behavior during the previous couple of years, the bursts of anger or emotion, the morbid entries I left in my mandatory journal in English class, the way I constantly hung around in the high school wing of the school rather than the middle school wing—which I, as a middle-schooler, was not supposed to leave. Maybe it was the time they sent me to the counselor, who visited the school once a month, because of my disturbing work in art class—which included holding a staple gun up to my head. But with almost all of this, I was able to make everyone relax. Because I was polite. Violent math book outbursts aside, for the most part I knew how to stay quiet about my home life. I wasn't told to not run my mouth; it was ingrained in me—was learned without having to be taught.

But when I hit Dave Stoll in the face with the math book, it was as if a bunch of women from the school—teachers, librarians, secretaries like Chad's mom—recognized my cry for help and suddenly banded together to help me change my life.

Or maybe it was that I wasn't as good at hiding my home life as I thought I was, and these women cared. Maybe even though my future was a mystery to myself, the end point of the path I was on was all too obvious to them.

WHEN THE BOARDING school pamphlets started to arrive at the house, my parents made no moves to stop me from applying. In fact, they encouraged the idea. Perhaps they knew there was a chance for things to get better between us if I left home. After all, a big part of why my test scores and grades were good was that my parents believed in books and education. And even though I was so bone-deep furious with my parents that I didn't want any part of anything they believed in, it was too late: I did the reading; I finished the homework; I wrote the essays. Not only was some kind of inextricable pride bound up in being a good student despite everything—and spitefully showing my folks that I could "do well" by their standards despite not doing well *at all* by almost any of their other standards—but I also had somehow internalized one of my family's ruling principles: Education can change your life.

It worked for my parents, eventually, although the change was a long time coming and the benefits—money, comfort, prestige, peace—didn't arrive until long after I was out of the house. And it worked for my half-sister, my father's daughter, Kerry, who didn't grow up with money but was smart and worked hard and got a scholarship to one of the best boarding schools in the country. I knew that, like me, she had been seeking independence from her circumstances. A chance.

The boarding school catalogs promised great educations, brilliant students and teachers, wholesome activities on manicured lawns. There were no cars up on cinder blocks, no holes punched into walls, no screaming parents surrounded by broken glasses and plates. I looked at those glossy pages and dreamed between the lines, too, imagining what leaving for school could give me—a way to get out of my house and out of my town and out of myself, to be able to leave behind all the parts I hated so that I could figure out what I wanted to replace them with.

The day my acceptance letter arrived, it came with the news that I'd also received a scholarship and financial aid package. A free ride. After opening and reading the letter I sat in the house alone, surrounded by the kind of jangly tinnitus-like silence that's left behind after six years of noise and anger and violence. I didn't cry, because the news was too big to cry about; I didn't know which part of it to react to. I just sat there. Realizing for the first time in my life that change was possible.

LIKE MANY THINGS that you dream will magically transform your life, my time at boarding school had a . . . challenging start. My friend Tommy drove me there in his truck and dropped me off, and I walked the rest of the way up the hill to the campus, my belongings in a couple of backpacks.

The dorm where I'd be living was a giant cinder-block building into which thirty or so fourteen-year-old boys were stuffed and watched over by a dorm parent, who was usually in his early twenties (which made sense to me at the time and seems slightly hilarious now). The dorm over-looked the school's idyllic playing fields and the rolling hills of Massachusetts.

The drive from my home to campus had taken about forty-five minutes, but I felt like I'd stepped through a portal to another galaxy. Like, a pretty fancy and intimidating one. My roommate was a tall blond from Cape Cod who had that easy-seeming aura of East Coast wealth, where the vibe was casual and nautical, moneyed in a way that was both uptight and relaxed, and utterly confident. He extended his hand and introduced himself as Jon Ritzman. I had never met anyone like him before.

In contrast, I was awkward, off-putting. Wearing beat-up sneakers with ripped jeans and a sweater despite the heat, hoping the wool made me look wealthier than I was. Trying to make a good impression while not trying too hard while having the sinking feeling that whatever charms and social skills I possessed back home wouldn't be readily transferable to a boarding-school setting.

As Ritzman made his bed, I unrolled my sleeping bag onto my mattress. I didn't have any sheets. Nor did I have a tie or jacket, which I found out were mandatory dress code for that night's formal dinner.

When I look back on how ill prepared I was, I can't really remember *why*. Surely the school would have sent some kind of list of the things I was expected to bring. And if so, okay, my family was poor, but it didn't seem like a huge stretch for them to spare some sheets (like from the bed I'd no longer be sleeping in) and a jacket and tie handed down from my father or bought for a few dollars or less from a thrift store or church sale. Why would my parents let me go off to boarding school like this? Did they not know? Did they not *care*? Or, just as likely, had I refused any and all help?

Years later I'd read *The Secret History* by Donna Tartt—set at a college so clubby and small that sometimes it felt more like a terrifyingly zero-rules boarding school—and come across this description of that poor, doomed asshole Bunny Corcoran:

> What the Corcorans did with their sons was to send them all to the most expensive schools they could possibly get into, and let them fend for themselves once they were there. His parents don't give him a cent. Apparently they never have. He told me when they sent him off to Saint Jerome's they didn't even give him money for his schoolbooks. Rather an odd child-rearing method, in my opinion—like certain reptiles who hatch their young and abandon them to the elements.

Keep in mind that in the world of this novel, it's considered absolutely outrageous for a parent to not give their kid an allowance when they're in college, and if they didn't it was a direct attack made out of pure spite (although the narrator himself had a work-study job and finds this state so distasteful it feels like a secret even to himself).

Anyway, for whatever reason, I didn't have a jacket and tie, and my roommate kindly and breezily lent me his, because of course he had multiples of each.

I put on the slightly too-big jacket. The tie I kept gripped in one hand. Then, when there was nothing else left to do, I took the tie and wrapped it loosely around my neck, like some kind of stylish (I hoped) fucked up (I knew) scarf-cravat-thing.

". . . Oh," Jon said. "Let me help you."

AFTER I GOT settled, once I had a free moment, one of the first things I did was walk into town. I had to buy a tie. And a jacket. And some sheets. Which meant I needed money. Hence, I needed a fucking job. In the center of town, I passed a Cumby's with a Help Wanted sign out front. Cumby's was short for Cumberland Farms, which was a New England chain of 7-Eleven-esque convenience stores. I went in and applied, instinctively knowing that it was of the utmost importance to hide the fact that I was a student at the boarding school. It worked. I got the job.

Later I'd learn that the students and even some of the faculty referred to the local residents as "townies." I lived less than an hour from campus in a way crappier town, and for the full four years at school, I had this label stuck right onto my secret heart of hearts— even after I learned how to fit in with and befriend the other students, so many of whom were inordinately well-off, though a few were scholarship kids like me, or day students who lived in the surrounding area. No matter. My whole time at school, I knew what I really was: a townie who'd crossed over.

When I told my dorm parent that I'd gotten a job at Cumby's, he looked surprised for a moment, before laughing his ass off. He said good on me, but that just wasn't going to fly. Students were supposed to be here to be students; they weren't supposed to get jobs off campus and confuse everyone and squander time away from their studies. It was arranged that I could do odd jobs in the dish room and cafeteria and the school bookstore in exchange for cash.

BOARDING SCHOOL WAS a contradictory environment, a place both soft and hard, cruel and kind. It was everything, and it was a lot of it.

In some ways, the dorm could have beeen considered worse than the house I'd left behind: a fully institutional building with walls made of cement bricks painted dull white, illuminated overhead by fluorescent lights. Yet I loved it for not being my house, for being full of people who weren't my family, whose yelling and screaming couldn't wound me—at least not in the same way my parents' could.

Plus, we all had our own phones and computers, which was a first for me. Most kids had laptops or candy-colored iMacs, but I was happy just to have a computer at all, even if it was an old beige tank that sounded like it was in actual pain when you started it up.

Though I thought I was going to boarding school purely for the academics, sports turned out to be a big deal here, too, particularly the well-funded hockey program. The rink was high up on a hill, as if to confirm the importance of athletics at this school relative to academics, and that hockey was the most important sport of all. When some friends on the varsity team learned that I couldn't skate (my time on the ice had come to an early and abrupt end after my father accidentally kicked me in the head with a skate when I was a little kid), they took me up the hill, strapped me into skates, and didn't quit until I knew how to glide forward with ease and backward with, well, a little less ease, but it got the job done.

We also played football—all of us, our freshman year. The school encouraged it, and we didn't know what else to do. Since we were fourteen-year-olds in the year 1997 we thought it'd help make us popular. One of my friends was so small that his helmet had to be special ordered. At that age we all were growing in wildly varying skips and stutters; some of us looked like children and some of us looked like near-adults, and somehow all of us were fourteen. My friend looked like a child, but when he broke his arm during practice, none of the coaches believed him. Instead they told him to suck it up, so he kept playing.

Surrounded by superjocks, I began to obsess over my body even more than I had before. When I started boarding school, I was not the fattest kid around, or even the fifth fattest, but I was big enough for, say, Dave Stoll to call me "tubby." That all changed as the years went by. Some of it was growing up and losing a bit of baby fat. I was also simply moving more—not just playing sports but going on runs and training the way the athletes and so many of the other students did. And some of it was, well, that I started taking the pharmaceutical speed my new friends would give me for free.

I hadn't wanted to admit it, but I had been worried that I couldn't handle the increased workload of an intimidating private school. Mere months into my freshman year, friends had taught me how to use my new school ID card to crush up the pills before snorting them. "Diet Coke," we liked to call it. By my senior year, my ID card was worn, bent, and stained with various pill pastels, and I was putting more than one hundred milligrams of Ritalin and Adderall up my nose a day.

The summer before I left to start boarding school, I had tried with varying levels of success to lay off booze, cigarettes, and especially drugs, since I figured boarding school would be less drug focused and more strict.

It turned out that rich kids did drugs just like poor kids (they did what they could get) and they also did drugs just like rich kids (they did what they wanted to get). Their parents had sent them to expensive doctors, who prescribed them these pills that were supposed to help them focus, make them act up less. The school nurses would dole them out like it was some kind of Pink Floyd video or a rich-kid version of *One Flew Over the Cuckoo's Nest*, because that's how it felt to these kids, because screw their parents for settling for what was often a Band-Aid solution to deeper issues and trying to alter their moods and minds.

The son of a famous baseball Hall of Famer bought us dip. We smoked cigarettes furtively in the woods. We bought cans upon cans of Glade air freshener to huff in our dorm rooms—we bought so many that we cleaned out the entire Star Market downtown—doing this whole routine where we pretended to be snooty waiters with towels over our arms, saying shit like, "Ah, yes, a can of the purple, with notes of purple Nerds, sir, a very fine choice," before putting the towel over the top of the can and spraying and inhaling until we passed out. We crushed and snorted the aforementioned pills and a few other kinds; we got liquor and weed and shrooms and acid. Rich kids did drugs like it wasn't a referendum on their whole entire future, like they weren't proving they were trash just like everyone knew they were.

When I first came to the school, I thought all rich people were assholes and poor people were saints. It's still a good rule, all things considered, but my time at the school allowed me to realize that sometimes, rich people could be good people too. And as my views broadened, I would go back home to see my old friends some weekends and would realize, through their actions and the language they used, that some of them were really just assholes too. Money doesn't make you who you are.

I THOUGHT I was adjusting, adapting, growing. Sanding that chip off my shoulder. But visiting home reminded me that this also meant I was changing.

I didn't know if I wanted to be changed. Of course I missed my old friends, who came from where I came from and knew about me and my parents, and whose worlds had been just about the same size and shape as mine. I tried to stay at friends' houses or visit my half brother at UMass Amherst, and avoided going back to my parents' house at all costs. My parents were arguing less—I'm sure me being out of the house helped—but the tension was still there, the anger still there. The resentment, this emotion none of us could manage to put down. Each of us resenting the others for things we were never going to be able to change, none of us willing to think about the future while letting go of the past. But for the most part, back at home I felt *at* home, hanging out at Connor's or Tommy's, smoking weed and working on cars, driving fast through the hills where I lived.

At the same time, I'd come to thrive on the feeling of being set into a far bigger container—one whose possibilities I was growing into, with still more room to move.

So I learned to switch. Visiting home, I'd slip right back into my country ways. Coloring lines on my cigarettes with black sharpie markers (we called them "zebras," and the effect wasn't all that different from inhaling Glade air fresheners). Drinking around campfires, lighting off fireworks, shooting at my friends with BB guns and at empty beer cans with real guns, throwing anything with an edge at trees out of boredom. Fast cars, danger, fire, and knives.

And yet I instinctively knew how to act when boarding school friends would take me to New York, where we'd stay at their families' pieds-à-terre, which is a French term meaning "incredibly fancy apartment in the city that goes completely unused 99 percent of the time so that rich shithead kids can trash it." One of them was so high up and close to the Met that if we threw a rock from the balcony of the penthouse apartment it would have gone through the glass ceiling of the museum. There were snorkeling trips to Florida, spring breaks in Miami and Fort Lauderdale (the latter reminding me more of my home, a trashy place where I felt comfortable). A friend's father was a doctor who did work on Nantucket, and we flew out to the island on his private plane with him. High in the air above the ocean, he let me take the controls.

Did I sometimes feel like a charity case? Sure, but I would take it. I couldn't pass up the chance to experience something other than all I'd known for the first fourteen years of my life. Also, I realize now, I was getting a crash course in a particular set of social skills. Everything involved when you make real friends you love and care about and vice versa, and then they want to bring you along to places and do things that blatantly remind you, "Damn, we sure did grow up different." I knew how to be a good guest—grateful, but not too grateful. Making my presence as light and not burdensome as possible without being servile. I knew when to ask questions and reveal my ignorance or inexperience, and I knew when to shut up. I knew how to be delightfully working class, to tell entertaining stories that didn't make the listeners feel guilty or freaked out about what the hell kind of scary hick their kid had brought on vacation. And, while for the most part everyone was kind and generous to me, I learned to ignore when I had been (usually) inadvertently insulted or condescended to and how to smooth it all over.

I loved both of my lives, and for a long time I felt content to keep them separate. Most likely I thought that was the only way it'd work. However, in the later years of high school, feeling more confident in my boarding school life, I relaxed a little.

I started to bring friends back to where I grew up. Often they would stay with me at my friends' houses, my world as strange to them as their world had been to me. The first time Jordan Kemler came for the River Rat Race. Every year, two old mill towns had a canoe race down the river. A great excuse to get drunk and have fun, though some took it seriously, cutting through the water in sleek, fast canoes.

But mostly we would just drive around like maniacs, drunk, doing donuts and using the e-brake to take corners far too fast on roads I knew like the back of my hand, hitting the minor bumps at just the right speed to take the car briefly, wondrously airborne. One time, the police showed up and I watched as my friend from boarding school was put into the back of a cop car. Me and my hometown friends had had so many run-ins with the law that we knew most of the officers by name. It was a small town and, as I've said, white as hell. We had that privilege going for us.

The second time Jordan visited, we went to a party where kids from the neighboring town showed and started an all-out brawl. I got my ass beat, dried blood and bruises on my face lingering the next day. The kids from the neighboring town had started the fight because they said this kid Terry had felt up one of their sisters while she was passed out at a party. Terry was in the theater club, came up about as high as my chest (and I wasn't tall). He didn't seem like he'd hurt a fly; we knew him. He had this legendary story about the time he worked at the dump smashing toilets. On his first day of work, his boss demonstrated for him, taking a sledgehammer to a row of toilets, one detonation of white porcelain after another, until he reached one toilet that exploded both white and brown. He just whipped his face to the side and said, flat and deadpan, "Welp, shit in that one," before continuing on down the line of toilets. We said "Welp, shit in that one" all year. So we protected Terry.

The night of the party, as the whole scene devolved into flailing punches and vicious kicks, I found myself collapsed over Terry. Not so much defending him, as taking his licks for him. The fists and kicks hitting my face and ribs seemed to last forever until some more friends joined the fray and fought the other kids back into their cars. A brawl was nothing new, but I felt a weird sense of pride in knowing that it was the first fight Jordan had ever witnessed that wasn't during a hockey game.

Months later I'd find out from a buddy that Terry had actually felt up that girl while she was passed out at a party. He was a total fucking creep whose beating I had taken for him. I felt sick.

"I didn't want to tell you," my buddy said. "Because I know you stuck up for him, but . . . you picked the wrong guy, man."

I couldn't bring myself to tell Jordan until years later that we had been on the wrong side of history.

BY THE TIME I got to college in Washington, D.C., living in dorms was second nature. As my college classmates reveled in their newfound freedom, I did the same thing I'd done when I'd gotten to campus in high school: I went out and got a job. This time, I got to keep it.

I find that my time in college just isn't as memorable as the years I spent in boarding school. Don't get me wrong: I loved college, too. I lived in the honors dorm my freshman year, which turned out to be a housing error, but when I got an email the summer before saying there'd been a mistake, I wrote back from a fake email address pretending to be my father and threatening to pull myself from the school if they didn't let me stay. That said, I also remember arriving at my freshman dorm and asking where I could get some Ritalin or Adderall. A kid on the eighth floor, someone told me. When he tried to charge me twenty dollars I laughed. I couldn't believe people paid money for study drugs at college. Then I struggled the most I've ever struggled trying to write my first paper for class. But I got used to the lack of free "Diet Coke" and pulled down good grades and eventually graduated with honors. This while partying, marching in anti-war protests with the black bloc, and throwing a chair through a Starbucks window, as well as working twenty to forty hours a week at the school library, in bars and restaurants throughout the city, and, one summer, helping my boss with his fish tank business out of Southeast D.C.

If I sound like I'm bragging, I am. I was proud of myself. I felt like a complete person, like someone who had practiced and trained and worked to squeeze the very most out of life. Because of my time at boarding school, college came easily to me. Because of my time working various jobs since age twelve, balancing work and my studies came easily to me. That doesn't mean I wasn't tired sometimes, or that I didn't occasionally drop a few balls. Still, I always knew I could get it all done. Maybe *that's* why I don't find college so memorable: Unlike all the years before, it did not give me anything harder than what I could already handle. Even socially, college, it turned out, was no match for the focused and terrifying and wonderful immersion of boarding school, the way all its sudden strangeness and alienation bloomed outward into brand-new joys and terrors and challenges.

Though to be honest, another reason I might not remember college so well is that I was partying more than ever, getting into drugs like cocaine. By the time graduation day rolled around I was passed out, as I so often was, on the floor of the small apartment I shared with an old friend who had long since grown sick of my shit. He was kind enough to kick me awake on his way out the door to meet his family who had driven down for the ceremony.

My parents had also made it down, which I felt conflicted about, and which probably factored heavily into my decision to spend the day before their visit getting absolutely obliterated (a habit that would last well into my thirties).

Graduation took place outside near the National Mall, in sight of the White House and many other monuments. It was a hot, clear day, and I was drunk off the champagne and orange juice and vodka and orange juice I had brought with me and shared with my classmates, and was smoking cigarettes and trying not to pass out in the heat. Afterward my parents, obviously pissed that I was visibly drunk, posed for a few pictures and then took off. I was feeling manic and can't remember much.

That summer, I stayed in D.C. to keep working at the Department of Justice, in the Civil Rights Division, helping with Americans with Disabilities Act cases. Those days, I found myself more often than not in a bar.

"Isaac!" someone said behind me.

It was a friend, or a friend of a friend. We talked, caught up on some things. The bar was about to close.

"Hey, my place is right around the corner," he said. "Come over for one more drink, I want to show you something."

We walked over to his place. He pointed to a photo on the mantel above his purely decorative fireplace. It was him on graduation day with two people, I assumed his parents.

"Do you remember taking that?" he asked.

I shook my head, even though a memory of grabbing a nice camera from someone dislodged itself tentatively from the dustbin in my brain.

"That's me with my parents. They'd gotten divorced when I was a kid and they both remarried. Started new families pretty quick."

I nodded. I was wondering if maybe we were drunker than we thought.

"Every photo I have is with them and their new families. And I get along with them, of course. But what I'm trying to say is, other than when I was a baby, I never had a photo of just me and my mom and my dad. Your drunk ass at graduation, you just grabbed the camera from my mom, shoved the three of us together and snapped the photo. Handed the camera back and started taking other families' photos. It was a whirlwind and you were gone. Even as I got the film developed I wondered if it'd come out. But it did. And now it's my favorite photo."

I appreciated what he had told me more than I could say. For what it was worth, I had internalized my parents' disapproval of me on graduation day, had filed that occasion away as yet another one I'd ruined for them. I told my mother later about the photo, hoping she might see something besides my drunkenness—how everybody was just trying to capture that moment, a moment of happiness.

She didn't really get it, but at least I could keep and hold another perspective of the day. The day that I had finally accomplished what my family had always wanted me to do: better myself. Improve my life through books and education and getting into the same rooms as the rich people. Though I had to get away from them in order to do this, and though for a long time I stayed away and we were near-strangers to each other, this whole time all I was doing was becoming ever more fully their son.

Hold Steady

The first time I listened to the Hold Steady, I was committing low-level health insurance fraud and mopping a floor in a hotel on an island ten miles off the coast of New Hampshire.

Now, when I say "listened," I mean really listened. Not just heard, since I know I must have heard the Hold Steady before—the music was playing on an old iPod that my college friends had filled with their favorite albums and given to me earlier that year. My friends were cooler than me, which would always be true at any time in my life. (I tend to punch above my weight when it comes to friendship.) After my buddy Josh got a new iPod Mini, they gifted me his old, clunky white one, deciding once and for all that I needed to learn about music, because I barely knew anything and man, was it breaking everyone's hearts.

I had always been music-dumb. While I liked listening to it just fine, my tastes were completely haphazard, a grab bag of every random tune fate had thrown my way. I had tapes I'd gotten when I was a kid—the White Album and *Appetite for Destruction*—which my half-brother had made for me by holding a tape recorder to his father's record player. I listened to 107.3 WAAF, the only station I could get on my alarm-clock radio, the cheesy post-grunge drowning out my parents' fighting. The only CDs I owned were Silverchair's *Frogstomp* and the Goo Goo Dolls' *A Boy Named Goo*, both of which I'd stolen from the brand-new Walmart in the next town over. Unfortunately, I hadn't bothered to steal a CD player, which made listening to the albums rather hard.

By the time I got to college, I still had the CDs, plus a random array of MP3s on my hand-me-down laptop. I listened to music but never embraced it—I didn't hide my ignorance, but I didn't seek out anything new either. Of course, this drove my friends insane. They didn't want me to just consume music like junk food, like something that could be anything as long as it got the job done. They cared about music and wanted me to care too. I think they must have decided to give me Josh's old iPod the day one of them, Big Pete, saw me lugging my giant, weighty laptop around in my backpack with a headphones cord snaking out of the zipper.

"Isaac," Pete said, with dawning horror. "Have you been carrying around your laptop all day just to listen to your shitty MP3s?"

". . . Yes?"

Fast-forward to the island off the coast of New Hampshire, to mopping the floor, to the impending insurance fraud, to *really listening* to the Hold Steady for the first time. The name of the album was *Separation Sunday*, and every song seemed to be sung right to me. How else could I have recognized so much of it? The low-stakes drug dealing, the accusatory hoodrat friends, the ER visits. Drinking gin from jam jars.

Separation Sunday was the kind of rock 'n' roll I'd been missing. Music that felt like an anthem crossed with a fistfight, a guided free fall—loud and cutting, but built with purpose. The singer sounded brash, both couldn't-give-two-shits and passionate by turns. Sometimes he'd twist his voice into something approaching tunefulness, even beauty; then he'd throw it all away to snarl, mutter, and shout. It was riveting.

I could see my past in the songs. My friends. Not the ones from college, so kind and generous with their iPods, but the ones back home, from a town called "Hostile, Mass." (a song I didn't know yet because my buddies hadn't put *Almost Killed Me*, the Hold Steady's first album, on the iPod). The characters in *Separation Sunday*—Holly and Charlemagne and Gideon—felt familiar. They were the people I grew up with; they were me. There were also plenty of references to Jesus and churches, enough to make me wonder if my friends had snuck a Christian rock band onto the iPod as a joke. But, fuck it, I decided. If this was Christian rock, then, I guess, I was into Christian rock now.

On the island, my job was mostly custodial with a little maintenance work. Not exactly what my parents were hoping I'd be doing after graduating from college and passing up an opportunity at the Department of Justice in Washington, D.C., because I was starting to realize that their idea of justice and my idea of justice differed. It was late in the summer, and I had come to the island to help with the last few hotel guests and then close all the buildings down for the season. It was a dependable job, one I'd been working on and off since I was sixteen.

I had arrived on the island the night before. When I got off the ferry, I was immediately greeted by friends. We did what friends working on an island do: We drank, and we drank some more, and eventually we ended up stealing a boat. Which we would argue was more like "borrowing," since we fully intended to return it when we were done. It was a small thing, a metal skiff, meant to get a few folks from island to island when the rowboats wouldn't do. Nothing like the fine sailboats rich vacationers moored in the harbor.

Jonny, one of my buddies, sat at the engine, steering us out past the breakwater and into the open ocean. I was drunk and bold and had no idea what I was going to do with the rest of my life but overjoyed to be back north after a brutally hot August in Washington. I stood at the bow, hands wrapped around a rope, laughing as our skiff bounced off the waves—which, as my buddy Dave pointed out, were pretty choppy that night and maybe it'd be best if I sat down. Not to mention that the water had made the metal slippery and my cowboy boots weren't helping.

I don't remember my face smashing into the bow of the boat, or falling backward, or my friends cutting the engine. I was just looking at the ocean one minute and the next, I was staring up at the stars, my back damp, somehow flush with the bottom of the boat. I sat up and felt blood warming my mouth and the front of my shirt. Jonny asked if I was okay, and I smiled at the absurdity of the question.

"Fuck, man," said Dave. My front tooth, which was already fake, was gone, leaving behind a black, blood-edged hole.

Under the full moon, we searched the murky water at the bottom of the boat for my tooth and couldn't find a damn thing. Finally, we gave up and decided that this was, perhaps, a sign to head for shore. Jonny gunned the engine. Slowly, the skiff crept back toward the dock.

The general consensus was that I should hide the injury until the next day. While staff didn't get official health insurance, there was a pool of money we all paid into that was used to cover on-the-job injuries, should they arise (which they inevitably did). I'd been paying into that pool since I was sixteen. As for the fact that I wasn't at work when I got hurt—that I had actually been drunk on a stolen boat—that just seemed like a technicality.

The next day, hungover and mopping a hardwood floor in a room where guests had performed a talent show the night before, having shoved my bloody shirt into a compost bin and kept my gappy mouth shut at breakfast, I was deep in the throes of falling in love with *Separation Sunday* (although maybe I'd have to check on the whole "Is this Christian?" thing) and not just the album but also the band itself, a band that would become that rarity for musically challenged me—a band that I followed and whose albums I'd seek out, who I would even see live despite my never going to shows (a hangover from growing up poor in a rural town, because who'd want to buy a ticket that cost more than three CDs, and who the fuck could even get you to the venue, anyhow?). I listened to the album on repeat and as "Cattle and the Creeping Things" kicked into high gear and my manager was nowhere to be seen, I thought, "This is it," and knocked over the bucket and threw myself down on the floor as hard as I could, my body starfished and prone, brown mop water seeping into my clothes.

My manager ran in. "Oh my god! What happened?"

"I don't know. I must have slipped," I said, actually a little dazed. (I might have overdone the throwing–myself–to–the–floor bit.)

"Isaac! Your mouth!"

I remembered the plan and flashed more of my remaining teeth, feigning shock as my hand went to my face.

"Wait, where is it?" my manager asked.

"What?"

"The tooth," she said, looking down at the floor. "Where'd it go?"

"Oh, man . . . I fell pretty hard . . . It must have . . ."—I fumbled, my brain completely cobwebbed from the night before—"broken into a million pieces?"

My manager looked at me; her face scrunched. She weighed the bullshittiness of my story against my very impressive pratfall plus the pain in the ass it would be to deal with me further. "Fine," she said.

From my headphones came the voice of Craig Finn, whose name I didn't even know yet, singing, "You came into the party with a long black shawl," as I picked the iPod off the floor and went to fill out an incident report in exchange for a new fake tooth.

A FEW YEARS after the tooth incident, I found myself working at a bar in San Francisco. I had traded the Atlantic for the Pacific after leaving a couple of jobs I shouldn't have left and being fired from some jobs that definitely should have fired me. The bar, which had once been a legendary biker bar and before that a legendary gay bar, had a stellar jukebox and was open from nine A.M. to two A.M. every day. It was the kind of workplace where I got reprimanded for smiling too much, never mind being nice to customers. There was a memorial wall with photos of bar employees who had died—like Steve, who hadn't been able to beat cancer for the second time, and the old owner, Hans, who'd been killed in a double murder. I was in my twenties, so I romanticized ending up on that wall someday. (If I'm being honest, I still do.)

Jef with one F manned the grill in the bar's kitchen and was one of the coolest co-workers I've ever had. He was covered in tattoos—on his forearm was a candle burning at both ends, the emblem of hard partiers who get shit done. He was more comfortable in his skin than anyone I'd ever met, a mishmash of a Midwestern sports fan who loved baseball even more than he loved getting fucked up and a punk rocker who was passionate about music writing. Jef wrote constantly about the shows he went to, in town and at festivals like South by Southwest. He kept it pretty quiet, but later in our friendship, when he finally told me he was a writer, I started to look for his stuff online. Though I usually didn't know what bands or venues he was talking about, I read on for the pleasure of Jef's idiosyncratic voice.

He was gay, often called me the F-word, and liked to fuck with my New England sensibilities just to watch me squirm. "It's okay, I can say that word. *You* can't, but I can," he'd tell me. Then, with a grin: "Not *yet* you can't, at least."

We'd drink until we felt comfortable talking about all the darker things, the bad memories we tried not to keep. And then we'd drink some more, to keep us from remembering what was said the next day, nodding to each other at work before starting it all again. We'd go to baseball games and ride our bikes together, day-drinking as we moved through the city with more swiftness and grace than we had any right to. Even if our legs wobbled and our balance was so shitty that barstools were not to be trusted, once we were up on two wheels everything was magically steady and smooth, as if our bikes were the better part of us. Jef rode everywhere. We all did.

"You wanna just play the Hold Steady?" Jef would ask from the kitchen while I cleaned the bar before the evening crowd showed up. Then he'd switch the music and turn it up loud. It was 2007 and the Hold Steady had come out with *Almost Killed Me* (2004), *Separation Sunday* (2005), *Boys and Girls in America* (2006), and would release *Stay Positive* the following year.

Like my college friends, Jef tried to teach me about the music he loved so much, surprised and amused by my ignorance. One time I asked him about the meaning of the letters LFTR PLLR, which were tattooed on his knuckles.

"Wait," Jef said. "Let me get this straight. You love the Hold Steady?"

"Of course."

"But you have *no idea* who Lifter Puller are?"

"No. Never heard of 'em," I said. There was a pause, and then I mumbled my usual, "I'm not great at music."

"Well," Jef said. "For someone who likes the Hold Steady so much, I just think it's funny you don't know Craig Finn's first band."

"Who's Craig Finn?"

Jef's laughter filled the empty bar.

"Come here," he said, motioning toward the jukebox. "I want to play you something."

Before Craig Finn was the lead singer of the Hold Steady, he was in Lifter Puller, along with Hold Steady bandmate Tad Kubler, from around 1994 to 2000. For all that time, and the first few years of the Hold Steady, Craig Finn had a day job; he didn't get to devote his time fully to music until he was thirty-three or thirty-four. Jef and I liked that. Jef was ten years older than me, and a year or two younger than Finn. It made us feel like we could still start working on our dreams tomorrow.

"He's spent some time in Boston, think he might have even been born there, like you," Jef told me. "But he's hardcore Minnesota, like me."

I can't remember if Jef was raised Catholic, but Finn and I were, which explained the religious themes in his lyrics. And it was amazing to hear Finn taking the world he knew and making art out of it. The band's music was attainable in a way we'd never been taught to expect. The songs operated as mirrors, reflecting our own experiences back onto us, even as they were windows, showing us how art could be made from the stuff of our lives—a world of misdemeanors and half-hearted escapism, through which real escape might be possible. The songs Craig Finn wrote were our stories, only better, and what more does one want from art but hope?

ONE DAY AT work Jef turned to me and asked, "Wanna go see the Hold Steady tonight?" I didn't even blink. "Hell yes!"

"Slow down," he said. "I can't go with you, I've gotta work. Plus I already went last night. Wait, did you not know they were in town?"

I tried to pretend my feelings weren't hurt.

"Oh, chin up, buttercup, I figured you knew. Here's the deal. I'm writing up the show, but I forgot to bring my camera last night, so I need you to go snap some pics tonight. Think you can do that?" He held out a ticket and a backstage pass to the Fillmore. The paper shone in the harsh, greasy light of the bar's kitchen.

"Wait," I said. "You write? I didn't know that."

"Bitch, there's so much you don't know about me it could fill AT&T Park. You in or not?"

I WENT HOME from the bar and got my leather jacket, the one nice thing I owned, which I'd bought at the Levi's flagship store in Union Square in the middle of a bender, benders being the only time that I really felt comfortable spending money on myself. I'd been bright-eyed and exhausted, trying to charm the salespeople, who probably didn't care whether I purchased the four-hundred-dollar jacket or not and just wanted me the hell out of the store. I had bought it because the leather was rich and brown and it fit my awkward body like nothing before ever had.

I peeled the backstage pass sticker from its backing and stuck it to the front of my jacket. Only later did I notice that everyone else had kept theirs hidden and just flashed it when necessary.

If there was one thing I knew less about than music, it was photography, but Jef had told me to get good shots of Finn, and I figured the closer I was, the better the shots would be. I squeezed my way forward until I was almost standing at his feet. Surrounding him were Tad Kubler on guitar, Galen Polivka on bass, Bobby Drake on drums, and Franz Nicolay on keyboards.

I was surprised to see Finn wearing a button-up shirt, a Grateful Dead dancing bear sticker on his baby blue guitar. He looked more suburban than I had expected, and it made me love him all the more. Here was a guy playing to a packed house at the Fillmore in San Francisco, and he looked like he had just dropped out of college and was surprised to find himself onstage.

Most of the people there looked more like Finn than like Franz Nicolay, who was the stylish, sharp-dressed one of the group. I was covered in sweat, both my own and everyone else's. The largely male audience—so emotional yet unaccustomed to displaying emotion—crushed up against me. Our bodies lifted one another up, and the physical sensation was a strange cross between fighting and hugging—minus the anger, plus a crowd. Dust floated in the spotlights as Craig Finn sang about dust floating in the spotlights.

That was the night I got it—the point of going to a live show. And for every feeling you could have at a show, well, there's a Hold Steady lyric for that. We all sang along at the top of our lungs, Jef's camera dangling against my side as I got caught up in the music.

After I got home, sweaty and beer-filled, I peeled the backstage pass off my leather jacket. I never did get up the courage to go meet the band, but it was enough just to have had the chance. I stuck the pass on my bedroom mirror to make sure I saw it every day, a reminder that music and art and writing could take you out of your world and into another, even if only for a night.

The next morning, I was nursing a hangover that had enveloped me like a heavy veil despite my attempt to thwart it by not sleeping. It was early in the morning, and the bar kitchen had just opened. I handed the camera back to Jef, who began clicking through the thumbnails right away.

"Isaac!" he yelled.

Immediately I thought I'd fucked up. "Did you know you took over seven hundred pictures? Jesus. I didn't even know it could hold this many." Jef started laughing, still looking through the photos. "Don't quit your day job, man. Half of these are of your feet. But I'll find something."

YEARS PASSED AND I was no longer working at the bar, though I still tried to get back as often as I could. Jef was employed at a few other places around town. Like anyone who's been in the service industry for a while, we were regulars at a bunch of spots—our new bars, our old bars, our friends' bars.

Eventually I got a job that kept normal hours, with real health insurance, even. The office was cramped and the work could be frustrating, but I poured my heart into it. My twenties were dwindling.

On the day I can't forget because I can't redo it, I took a phone call outside on the sidewalk. It was a sunny and hot July afternoon in San Francisco. I know the phone call was important—or more accurately, that I must have thought it was important—but today I couldn't tell you a single thing about it.

Someone said my name and I turned around.

Right away I knew something was off, because Jef wasn't riding his bike. Instead, he was walking it slowly down the sidewalk, leaning on it like a crutch.

"Isaac," he repeated.

It was early in the afternoon. "Isaac. Fuck you."

It was so beautiful out.

"Isaac. *Isaac.* Get the fuck off the phone. Let's go to the Five Hundred Club."

While I pretended to listen to the person on the other end of the line, my ears strained to turn each slurred sound Jef made into the word it wanted to be. Every word not even a word, but an inkblot of a word. I made the "cut it out" motion at him, my finger slicing my neck. My eyes flashing hot for a moment. I smiled, but it was strained. I needed this job. There was no time to go get drunk in the middle of the day.

He wouldn't leave, so I considered pushing him a little, something playful to get him off my back, but thought better of it. Swaying against his bike, Jef barely had the edge over gravity as it was.

"Fuck you, man," he said.

I plugged my finger into my ear and turned away, concentrating on the call. "What's that?" I asked the person I can't remember.

"Blow me," said the person I'll never forget.

As Jef walked away, he flipped me off with both hands behind his back, his bike perched neatly on his hip, never falling. A perfect feat of "Fuck you" pulled off with panache and grace, all from a guy who'd just been staggering a second ago.

They found Jef in his bedroom at the end of the week. It was July Fourth. The reason for his death felt like a nonanswer:

booze, partying, who knows? We gathered at the bar and put his picture up on the wall with all the others. Our family, our cemetery. We played the music Jef loved so much and played it loud. I couldn't bring myself to tell anyone about seeing him a few days earlier.

Six months later, I left San Francisco for Brooklyn. The reasons seemed simple: There was a job. And San Francisco had changed, the way San Francisco always does. It's a boom-and-bust town, and yet another tech gold rush had taken hold, one that seemed much more entrenched than the last.

But I'd be lying if I said it wasn't other things too. Going to my favorite bar, watching more and more friends go up on the wall. Walking that same block every day, regretting the dumb, douchebaggy finger I'd stuck in my ear as I turned my back.

It's not that I could have saved Jef. I've lost enough people to know that. You can't save someone when they're really going for it. That's like thinking I could have saved Steve, if only I'd just really put my mind to finding a cure for cancer. My sadness is only selfish: I could have hung up that phone and spent a few more hours or days (depending on how high we could stay) with my friend. We could have laughed together some more while Jef gave me shit. He would have smiled at me in his way that always made me feel loved, that made me feel like we were in it together even though we had no idea what "it" was, and I would have loved him back in my way.

We could have gone to a baseball game.

I HADN'T KNOWN that Craig Finn was releasing solo albums until a friend told me about *We All Want the Same Things*, which came out in 2017 (though, true to form, I was heinously late to the Craig Finn solo-album party, given that he'd put out his first in 2012). The album is beautiful in just the way I like, honest yet heightened, the mundane stuff of life transformed into storytelling. Everything busted and everyone trying their best. In one of my favorite songs on the album, "God in Chicago," Finn doesn't even bother singing. He just tells a story full of petty crime and stepped-on drugs and sadness. Two people pressing up against each other. Money that doesn't really amount to much—but it does for them. I've listened to this song again and again. It's a song that makes me cry, even though I can barely describe why, which of course makes me think about Jef who almost certainly could have. I wonder what he would think of Finn's solo work; I wish he could translate these records to me the way no one else could. How would Jef have grown over the years? How would he have developed as a writer? Would he have been able to write about these albums in a way that reached people, that got to the heart of what was worthy and wonderful about them?

Actually, I know the answer to that last question. Absolutely. Sure, Jef would have been critical, because he never liked giving anyone a pass. But I like to think he would have enjoyed the new characters, would have been able to illustrate the greater significance of Craig's stories, tackling things like PTSD and the opioid epidemic.

In the Hold Steady song "Stevie Nix," Craig Finn sings, "Lord, to be thirty-three forever," which I recognize as another one of those Christian references that made me so suspicious all those years ago, but thirty-three is also as a pleasantly comfortable age to want to be, weirdly attainable in a landscape of rock that's all about sixteen, seventeen, eighteen, twenty-seven at the most. But I can't even do that now—I'm way past thirty-three. I've grown up with Craig Finn's voice in my ears. I'm pretty sure I know where his albums end and my life begins, but I'm grateful that he so often blurs the line. That his music makes me feel like my friends and I live right there in those songs.

Not too long ago, I saw some of my college buddies. The ones who were so freaked out by my musical ignorance that loaded up Josh's iPod full of albums all those years ago, which is still one of the best gifts anyone has ever gotten me. Josh and his wife and their handsome baby were moving to Los Angeles, so we got together for a going-away party in New York City. We were all over the place at the time, but a bunch of us made it, up from D.C. and down from Massachusetts. Big Pete didn't show because he was about thirteen hours west of Nairobi doing aid work—but there was word that he'd visit that summer.

And me? I still visit Jef at the bar when I'm back in San Francisco, where his picture is up on the wall. I drink with him for a few minutes before going over to the jukebox. If they still have some of Jef's picks on there, I choose a song by Lifter Puller. I ask the bartender to turn it up real loud.

Home

The first time I saw Zeitgeist I was on a bike ride. I had just moved out to San Francisco to be with a woman who lived in a two-bedroom apartment with five people out in the Excelsior, "out past Silver," on the street where Jerry Garcia was born. After two days in cramped quarters with our noses pressed together, the woman suggested that I borrow her roommate's bike, so we could ride downtown and explore the city.

We rode down Mission Street over the highway and strained up one of San Francisco's many hills, receiving our immediate reward as we coasted downward, our wheels barely glancing against the road.

I didn't know it then, of course, but on this ride I passed so many places that would become second homes: the Knockout, a bar where I would end up selling sushi out of a beer cooler during Wednesday night happy hours; Blue Plate; Emmy's Spaghetti Shack (the old location); Zante Pizza & Indian Cuisine. Then we swung a left off Mission and onto Valencia Street and down to where it crossed Cesar Chavez (which still had the old name "Army" in parentheses next to it on the sign). At the intersection, high up on a billboard standing sentry over the Valencia Corridor, was the image of a giant California grizzly bear. It was an ad for a bank; I don't remember which one. The grizzly's teeth were bared.

Valencia Street was like none I'd seen before, lined with shops, great green hills overlooking it. We rode past 826 Valencia, a store selling pirate supplies where I would one day work, and numerous restaurants and bars and coffee shops that would become my haunts and their workers my friends. I was riding a bike through my future history.

I would experience love at first sight three times in San Francisco, the only place where that's ever happened, and the first time is the moment I saw Zeitgeist.

The woman and I stopped our bikes outside of a bar at 199 Valencia, a few blocks from where the two-mile street ends at Market. The sound of heavy metal surrounded us as a black door bearing the logo of a white skull with bunny ears swung open. On a stool sat a bouncer, a job that I would later have for too many years. The building itself was red and gray, with a high wooden fence encircling a beer garden. Before the door slammed shut, I caught a glimpse of a long, dark room filled with hesher-looking barflies. Tilting out front were motorcycles of all different makes, shapes, colors, and degrees of upkeep.

"That's Zeitgeist," the woman said. "You should definitely go there. I think you'll love it."

I already knew I did.

I LOVED BARS from the moment I first drank in one at fourteen, somewhere in Amherst, Massachusetts. My half-brother was on the rugby team at UMass. When I would visit him, I drank cans of beer with his teammates on the sidelines as we watched the players crash into each other with all the pent-up aggression and frustration of men who believe that they are only allowed to express one feeling.

After one match, we all headed to a bar downtown. I was worried that my usual "I'm a sophomore from Syracuse" lie wouldn't cut it. Especially since, now that I'm thinking of it, it was a lie absolutely nobody believed—except for the occasional tipsy undergrad who might pull me into dark and sticky rooms littered with Solo cups and menthols and kiss me while her friends hooted, and, now that I'm thinking about it, they were probably just pretending too.

"Don't worry," my brother—who was only eighteen himself—said. "They never check IDs. And even if they do, the bartender is a friend of the team's."

A bar felt like a whole new plane of existence, where drinking didn't have to be furtive or rushed or uncomfortable. Though I'd been drinking regularly since I was twelve, it was usually stolen bottles and cans downed hastily in the woods. Whether it was nighttime next to a shoddily built fire or midday by a pond or river, the beer was always the exact wrong temperature: warmish. But when I drank, I'd often think about how my parents didn't drink, and how they always seemed unhappy, and my mind connected these two facts, because I knew these bottles and cans always made me feel better, happier, lighter, even as they so often made me feel worse, and sadder, the next day.

And so this bar in Amherst glowed with possibility, this standard-issue, dark, wood-paneled room, forgettable as so many of them are, except the ones that mean something to you. How full it was of friends and future friends and companionable strangers, knocking glasses together and shouting for more. I sat, and a big bald man with a Viking goatee cried out, "Get the kid a Three Wise Men!" Plunked down in front of me was a single huge shot glass, which had three regular-sized shots poured into it: Jack, Jim, and Johnnie. I drank it like the kid I still sort of was, not knowing yet how to slam the liquor into the back of my throat. Instead, I tasted every drop as it rolled over my tongue, doing everything in my power to keep myself from wincing as the booze hit each new taste bud. The men cheered. There it was, the burn of a shot improperly taken mixing with the instant camaraderie of drinking.

At fourteen, in this place for adults, I immediately felt like a hero. My brother looked on proudly as another man yelled, "Make the wise men go hunting!" and an even larger shot was set before me. Jack, Jim, and Johnnie, with a shot of Wild Turkey poured on top. I swallowed it in gulps, the cheers of the men around me buoying my spirit as I did my best to keep everything down. Their love felt good, even if my body did not. The day began to fade into an amber-drenched late afternoon, all hazy with Camel Lights smoke and the fizzy ephemeral excitement of laughing with new friends, ones you might never see again—but that was part of the joy, wasn't it?—and all the other delightful things that come with day-drinking.

AFTER A MONTH of overstaying my welcome at my girl-friend's apartment in San Francisco—by, oh, a month minus one day—I found the place where I'd spend the next four years of my life.

The room was rough. It clearly had been meant as a laundry room, but the washer and dryer had never been installed; the other two renters had decided it'd be financially prudent to stuff a third roommate in there instead. Its one small window looked out over the hills south of the city, five television towers blinking in the distance. Despite living there for years I would paint only half of one wall, the barely used can of paint sitting next to my bed until the day I moved out.

After all, I didn't really need a place to hang out in and enjoy. Which was a good thing, because for all of us who lived there, the apartment was more like a storage locker where you could sleep or not sleep and shower before locking your shit up and getting out.

In fact, despite the lack of creature comforts and the abundance of, well, creatures—mice ran across the kitchen table while you were eating, as if you weren't even there, and pigeons nested in the walls—I was happy with my fetid room in my horrible apartment because it was located on McCoppin Street, a short block stuck right between Otis and Valencia, which meant that I now lived literally on the same block as Zeitgeist. And Zeitgeist could give me everything I wanted, all in one spot—a place to drink, talk, laugh, grieve, think. A place that comforted me with the old and familiar and exhilarated me with the fresh and strange. A place I worshiped and worshiped at.

This is what I had found in Zeitgeist. My perfect bar. My church. Open nine A.M. to two A.M. All day every day (save the one day a year they closed for cleaning). A place to call home.

WITHIN MY FIRST few weeks in San Francisco I got a job at Buca di Beppo (picture the Olive Garden but worse). Like any service industry job, it came with long hours, low pay, and the built-in camaraderie that comes with working for tips shoulder-to-shoulder with other people who are also selling overpriced pasta to tourists and listening to the same eight generic Italian songs play over the restaurant's sound system over and over again. To this day I still get tense if I hear "Che La Luna."

After work I'd get drunk with my co-workers at one of the many nearby Irish bars, where we'd try to wash the smell of marinara sauce off ourselves in the bar restrooms. Or I'd walk the two miles back to my apartment, avoiding the cost of public transportation, and sit in my room sipping on cheap beer while reading *Down and Out in Paris and London* by George Orwell, desperate to romanticize my meager living situation.

When I did have a little money, I would go to Zeitgeist. I loved the bar, and wanted to set myself up as a regular, enjoying a free drink every once in a while if one of the bartenders recognized me. But it wasn't simply my love of the bar that kept me coming back. A few of the other waiters at Buca had told me that the tips at Zeitgeist were some of the best in the city. Plus you didn't have to wear a uniform.

When you live a small life it's important to have small dreams. Working at Zeitgeist was mine.

THE BAR ITSELF is a long, dark room attached to another back room. In the back is a pool table, a couple of pinball machines, and a window through which you can order some of the best burgers in the entire city. The beef happens to be grass-fed and free-range and organic and all the other fancy modifiers, which both makes sense (San Francisco) and doesn't (Zeitgeist's aesthetic is metal bar meets dive bar meets German beer garden—not just in how it looks but in the workers' attitudes).

The two floors above the bar contain the cheapest residential rooms to be found in all of San Francisco, especially in the Mission district—SRO rooms, with shared bathrooms at the end of each hall—many of which are rented by the employees of the bar. Because on top of everything else Zeitgeist is a combination of, it's also got a powerful Californian Wild West vibe. No saloon-style swinging doors, but rooms right above the bar, it's got.

If you take a left at the end of the bar you'll find double doors that lead to a big wooden porch, which spills out onto an even bigger open yard. The ground is covered in gravel and the entire space is filled with massive wooden tables like one might find in a German beer hall. There's no service outside—you want a drink, you go to the bar. On warm, sunny days, the backyard can fill up by the beginning of the afternoon, and even earlier on the weekends.

On one outside wall there's a painting of four or five pink elephants precariously stacked, one atop the other, all balanced on a tiny motorcycle. Plants and trees are scattered throughout the yard. Sitting among them is a rusted-out tow truck, which we used to have to check frequently just to make sure nobody was having sex in the cab, or, as was more likely, passed out in it.

In the left back corner of the yard, there are three bright teal Porta Potties that serve as sad, smelly, graffiti-covered backups for the two single-use restrooms inside the bar. As if the backyard is some sort of festival that never ended. Next to them is a mural—a modern take on Botticelli's *The Birth of Venus*, less Renaissance and more goofy cartoon. Replacing Venus is a gray-haired, bearded dude with a big beer belly and a lei of flowers around his neck who modestly covers his man boobs with an arm and shields his crotch with a bottle of Dickel. That same wall is shared with Black Heart Tattoo, where over the years I'd get way more work done than I could afford.

"WHAT'S DICKEL?" I asked the man behind the bar.

I had lost my job at Buca di Beppo. In hindsight I'm sure all the time I was spending at Zeitgeist didn't help, but drinking wine on the job was frowned upon too. I'd lived in San Francisco for over a year now, but I wasn't going to make next month's rent. I had dropped off résumés at restaurants and bars all over town, including at least five at Zeitgeist, but nobody was hiring.

The truth was starting to sink in: I was going to have to move back East. The money was gone. The relationship I'd moved here for was over. Although I'd done my best to get a foothold in this marvelous, expensive city, my efforts had come up short. If I was lucky, my half-brother would be able to give me work at one of the numerous burrito shops he had been opening and running while I was busy drinking away my early twenties. Maybe it wouldn't be so bad. New Hampshire was a charming state. I loved my brother. Maybe if I was really lucky, I could work in one of his shops near the sea.

"What's Dickel?" the bartender heckled me. "You've been coming into here for how long now and you don't even know what Dickel is?" His voice was raspy and his name was Todd Thumm, aka "Happy Todd," named thusly because he had been voted Crankiest Bartender in San Francisco by the *SF Bay Guardian*.

Multiple times.

Todd poured me a shot. It just looked like a shot of whiskey, but a shot of whiskey was a lovely thing—the oily gleam floating on the surface, the burnished topaz below.

"This, *dipshit*, is Dickel. It was Hans Grahlmann's favorite whiskey."

"Who's that?"

Todd squinted at me. But his cranky look faded away as he couldn't help himself from launching into an old favorite story. "*Hans*. He owned this bar!"

Owned a bunch of bars all over the Bay Area, and in Hawaii too. Back before Zeitgeist was Zeitgeist it had been the Rainbow Cattle Company, a gay bar that Hans opened in 1977. In 1986, he renamed it Zeitgeist and shifted the bar's focus toward motorcycles. Though motorcycles were a true passion of his, it was a decision he'd been forced to make— Hans, like so many others, was struggling to keep his business afloat as San Francisco (and the world) was devastated by the AIDS epidemic and his friends, lovers, and community were suffering and dying all around him.

Goes without saying that Hans was a character unto himself. "He loved to piss people off!" Todd exclaimed, clearly finding a kindred spirit in the man. "He would go into gay bars that he owned and act like the most uptight German you ever met in your life, and then he'd go into his straight square-crowd bars and act like the biggest queen. He loved pushing people's buttons."

"Is he still around?" I asked, thinking maybe I could convince this extremely chaotic lovable asshole-sounding character to give me a job.

"Hans? No. No, he is not 'still around.' He got shot up near Guerneville. They never got the person who did it, either."

Other than me and Todd, the only other person in the bar was a homeless man sitting at a high table in the back corner, doing his best to stay warm. It was one of those days in San Francisco, a city that doesn't see too much rain, but when it does it's like it's spending all of its money at once. The way I was doing at Zeitgeist. It was my special kind of Me Math: If there wasn't enough money to make rent, then I might as well blow what I had on enough booze to make the problem go away for a while. Today was day two of my bender. A real wraparound—after closing the place down the night before, I was the first customer through the door this morning.

Todd had never talked to me this much before, this nicely—well, if nicely wasn't exactly the right word, then at least it wasn't *not* nicely—and I was enjoying the attention, the story, and the fact that the story behind this bar, which I so adored, was suddenly, through Todd, unfolding and opening up to me. It was like finding secret rooms in a house I already loved, a boozehound Narnia. Of course a place like this had an incredible history. All mythical places did.

So, naturally, that was when I made a big mistake.

"Well, listen," I said, as I ordered another drink, doing my best to sound like a comrade in arms. "I'll gladly spend the day here. I ain't got shit to do anyways. Happy to keep you company, just in case . . ." I nodded my head back in the direction of the man who had been nursing his beer for the past few hours, clearly here from the encampment right around the corner under the overpass on Thirteenth street.

"What?" Todd blinked like he had awoken from a trance, immediately transforming into a different person, which is to say the same person he had always been to me before today: grumpy, thorny, skeptical. "What do you mean?"

I had no excuses, only reasons. I desperately needed a job. I knew nobody at Zeitgeist started out behind the bar, you had to pay your dues working the door and the backyard. Security. And I was a young man in his early twenties, so I was a member of one of the planet's overall dumbest populations of people. Finally, since I'd spent part of my childhood in a homeless shelter, I felt like it gave me a pass, of sorts, though it did not. Especially if the person you were talking to had no inkling of your past, hadn't even fully registered your existence until today.

"You know . . ." I said, suddenly realizing how much I didn't want to finish the sentence. I had the sick recognition that I had overstepped my bounds, been overeager and desperate and tricked myself into making stupid assumptions about Todd and the homeless man and Zeitgeist, and now I was locked into saying something that I didn't even believe to be true, or at all fair. But I continued weakly, "I'm here. In case he starts acting weird. I have your back."

"Oh, *fuck* you," Todd spat, and turned his back to me. "Much more likely that some young jammer like you who can't handle his booze is gonna give me trouble than that man over there who's just trying to stay dry. *Dick.*"

The rest of Todd's shift, I overtipped, even though I couldn't afford it. Didn't matter. He didn't speak to me again. In silence he picked up money and turned it into alcohol that I drank.

I HAVE ALWAYS felt safe in bars. It's something I don't think about too much because it is simply the truth. Such a part of me. It's been that way since that first bar in Amherst. I think it has something to do with togetherness with strangers and familiarity with the rules. I can walk into any bar in this country, and many around the world, and for the most part I'm going to know how to act. What the baseline etiquette is.

This is true of the bars I ended up working at in college, one of which catered to students looking to get blackout drunk on a Tuesday, and the other, which took after an English-style pub, and catered to the parents who would visit campus on the weekends. And it was true of the bars I worked in after college, too, including Zeitgeist. It is also true of yuppie bars in Connecticut, all polo shirts and boat shoes, sailing rope glued around the edges of bathroom mirrors, or outdoor ice houses in Houston, Texas. Bars gave me a playbook to follow. After a childhood home with ever-changing rules and shifting emotional sands, a place built on stability, on nonobligating camaraderie, feels like a comfort to me. Pay your tab, tip your bartenders, and you can rest here awhile. Be as quiet as you want or as loud as is decent. This is a place where you can come and sit and be. Maybe even forget a trouble or two.

It's about taking up space on a barstool. I find safety in the simplicity. I sit there, money on the bar in front of me, and I drink. If you want to be with people, you can be with people. If you want to be alone, you can be alone. Say goodbye when you leave or quietly walk out the door. The choice is yours.

It's also about escape, of course. These little portals away from the outside world. A place that wraps a quilt around your brain for five dollars a glass. But for me it's also an escape plan. A safety net. Because I know how to tend bar. And I don't mean simply pour beers and shots, make drinks and talk to customers. I mean how to balance a till and wash floor mats and make setups and keep track of stock and close up. Because of that, whenever life gets a little dicey, I find myself thinking, "Maybe it's time to go work at a bar."

Anytime I walk into a bar for the first time when I'm traveling, I can't stop my mind from wondering, "What if I start a new life here? What would that future look like?" Bars aren't just portals of escape for me, they are millions of li'l centers of a million li'l universes, and I can imagine my life in each one. "What if this became my new center? My new universe?" And that's exactly what happened at Zeitgeist.

IT WAS A hot, gorgeous day in San Francisco, which I still called home, thanks to cobbling together enough money to live, sort of, from a retail job at the aforementioned pirate supply store where I was now an employee and early-morning work making and delivering sushi for a friend who was trying to get his catering company off the ground. At five A.M. every morning, I got up to cut fish that I would then drive to different tech campuses—Google, LinkedIn, Facebook—stocking their snack refrigerators with the hand-rolled fruits of my labor from a blue beer cooler. In my uniform of a black T-shirt and ripped jeans, and reeking of fish, I'd drag the cooler through brightly lit offices where everything matched except me. I skulked past stunning, well-dressed kids my own age having loud sex on top of piles of money. At least that's how I remember it.

My early twenties had quietly become my midtwenties and I still spent every dollar that didn't go to rent at Zeitgeist. Well, almost every dollar. Because now I'd been in SF long enough to stretch my bar legs up and down Valencia Street and sometimes deeper into the Mission.

So when I went over to Zeitgeist that day I knew the place was packed to the brim even before I saw it, the noise from the backyard crashing over the high wooden fence and onto the street. I peeked in just to be sure and saw lines of at least six people deep down the entire length of the bar. I simply shrugged and turned on my heel to head over to my second-favorite watering hole within a one-block radius of my apartment: Martuni's, a gay karaoke-martini bar that to this day sells Jacuzzi-sized martinis that hit you like controlled substances.

But before I could head out the door, someone shouted behind me: "Hey, you're the kid who wants a job here, right?"

I spun around to see a woman in her thirties in a black T-shirt, blonde hair tied back. "Uh, yeah!"

"Good," she said. "Get in here and start picking up glassware. We're slammed."

And that was my first day working at Zeitgeist. The first day of my many years there. That day, I was allowed to do only one simple task: I ran through the backyard, stacking glasses one on top of the other into a high, almost-toppling tower, held up by prayers and my shoulder, and then I brought the glasses inside, doing a fucked-up curtsey each time I passed through the doorway so the top of the tower didn't crash against it.

For hours and hours—actually, days and days—that was my entire job, tipped out by the bartenders at the end of each shift, not yet allowed to even wash the glasses, let alone pour a beer. Eventually, they started letting me watch the door.

What a job, I thought. On Sundays I started my shift at noon, the cheerful and lovely Elizabeth behind the bar, all tattoos and sunniness as she helped solve the problem of other people's hangovers (one of the T-shirts for sale read HANG-OVERS INSTALLED AND SERVICED), with Charlie—a ball of frenetic energy—barbacking for her. Two of my favorite people in the world. What a wonder to work in this cowboy heaven.

Which isn't to say people didn't give me shit, both as a form of love and to . . . give me shit. Mainly for two things:

1) Smiling: "Fucking stop being so nice!" Todd would yell, claiming it messed with his tips. How on earth, I thought at first, could being nicer to the customer get you smaller tips? Well, turned out he was right. At a place like Zeitgeist, with its reputation of toughness and cool, you kind of expect the staff to be comically surly—and you're disappointed when they're not. You want to feel a tiny bit scared and a lot excited, especially when you're one of those new-to-the-city tech kids with too much money and not enough life experience, desperate for someone to like you when they don't have to. And if they don't seem to like you, then you try throwing the money down to see if that does the trick. Within reason (and sometimes not), the worse you treat your clientele the better they tend to tip.

2) Wearing a button-up shirt: self-explanatory.

THOSE HOURS AND hours working at Zeitgest sometimes blurred together. As did the years. The ability to drink on the job was, of course, a big perk, but sometimes even alcohol couldn't move time in the right direction and it felt like you'd been working there for days on end, maybe longer if you'd also managed to smoke some weed during your shift. And then you didn't feel so much like those high walls in the backyard were protecting you so much as keeping you trapped inside, your eyes darting to the barbed wire on top that you never noticed when you were in a good mood. Bored at being on the job, we made our fun and talked to pass the time, telling stories, showing off tattoos, surrounded by people we loved—people with more nicknames than you could imagine or I could possibly list here.

Sometimes, when it was real slow, I would read. Paperbacks I bought at the used bookstore, Dog Eared Books, up the street. All the big drinking books, by big, loud men. And some sweeter ones, with more introspection. *The Tender Bar* by J. R. Moehringer, *A Drinking Life* by Pete Hamill. I dreamed of writing down my own Zeitgeist stories while reading the drinking stories of so many others. In a way, this was the same as reading *Down and Out in Paris and London*, or the books I had read as child about young protagonists who came from difficult homes. Life could be tough, but it could also be the stuff of legend. Maybe I could write legends of my own, even though I was often too drunk to write anything down.

Days and nights at Zeitgeist would weave themselves into one fuzzy, unending tapestry until something weird or wild or violent or sublime (or all of the above) snipped the thread, shocked us awake, made us elated to have a new story to share with the other workers and patrons.

There was the time the Hells Angels decided to put the bar on their blacklist, coming in one early morning and, over the course of an hour, stripping every Hells Angels–related sticker, poster, name carved into a table, and insignia from the bar, after which they walked out, never to return. When I asked the bartender, Cat—the Black woman who had somehow managed to piss them off simply by doing her job—what had happened, she responded, "Those fucking racist babies with bikes," and we both busted out laughing.

Or the night a bunch of cops came to the door, gave me the description of a man to look around for, but demurred when offered the chance to come inside and look around themselves.

There were scuffles and skirmishes, but my job mainly involved knowing how to talk someone who'd over-served themselves out of being a real fucking asshole, and occasionally rushing an idiot out the door by the scruff of their neck if they'd ultimately decided, "No, I *would* like to be a real fucking asshole."

There was the guy who spent twelve hours straight in the bar, nursing one beer and then slowly ordering another, leaving no tip. Obviously on hallucinogens, or so we thought. Finally, after another epoch had passed and he had made it to his third beer, Jerry, a bouncer with a calm manner, slowly walked up behind the guy and gently said, "Hey man, I think you've had enough."

"What's your name?" asked the man, who hadn't turned around, still facing his empty glass. He spoke slower than he drank.

"Jerry," he said, as he rested his hand on the man's shoulder, "and I think it's time—"

The "for you to leave" never made it out of Jerry's mouth. The man who had spent half a day moving like a tortoise whipped around and before anyone could react—as if he had been saving up all of his speed for this one moment—smashed his glass onto Jerry's head. The glass exploded, blood gushed, and we were all on the man, dragging him out the door as he punched wildly and screamed. But before anyone could really get started, Jerry joined us outside, his blood dripping on the pavement.

"Leave him alone," he said. "He's just a fucked-up old man. Now, who's gonna take me to the hospital?"

WHICH IS TO say, just like in the house I grew up in, Zeitgeist had violence too. Most bars do. But then again, you know why people are fighting in a bar. They are drunk. There's a method to the madness. My childhood home had none.

That said, method or no, there was still a lot of madness. I could tell you all the stories about celebrities visiting Zeitgeist—I will always regret not getting into a taxi with John Waters—or the local celebrities who were always shown more love than the big-name out-of-towners. The motorcycle clubs who came by weekly, or monthly, or annually, depending on which club we're talking about, or the lone bikers who sat in the corners, never seeming to leave. The nights spent doing coke upstairs with bike messengers and having sex in the SRO bathrooms after a shift of telling people not to do coke and have sex in the bathrooms below. The history of the Rainbow Cattle Company and how it was a haven for members of the LGBTQ community who moved to San Francisco in the seventies and early eighties, an old-timer once telling me, "You used to be able to slide from right here all the way to the back of the place, just on the cum."

But these are all stories that are best told over beers at a bar like Zeitgeist. Which is what we so often did. Working there, I quickly formed bonds that went past co-workers and dove from a high height headlong into friendship and sometimes more. While often, like Todd, we presented as gruff, the friendship (and a healthy amount of drugs and alcohol) also allowed for moments of vulnerability. Drinking can help you hold down your emotions, until it becomes the crux that allows you to let them bubble up too.

In hindsight, it seems so obvious to me. My father didn't drink. So I spend a lifetime finding refuge in bars. Finding companionship in bars. Finding the father figures I didn't know I was searching for in bars. Zeitgeist, a place of bikes, both the bicycles of bike messengers and the motorcycles of everyone else. At the time I couldn't see how that related to my father either, but there were those childhood days in Boston, him running along the Charles River while I rode my bike beside him. Or my sadder days in North Central Massachusetts, riding my bike to the center of town, alone but grateful to be out of my house. I equated bikes with happy memories of my dad and with childhood freedom. Of course I loved a bar that put them front and center.

Zeitgeist was a wonderful place to run away to, a West Coast escape to work on all the trauma I'd built up on the East Coast over my first twenty or so years of life. Well, maybe not so much as "work on" as "bang at" it with a bike wrench in one hand and a jar full of beer in the other . . . but in my humble and not at all educated opinion? That's an important part of the work too.

THE BAR BECAME my family. Thanksgiving. Christmas. For almost a decade, I didn't go back East for the holidays. I celebrated at Zeitgeist. Giant turkeys and delicious ham to eat, pinball and pool and beer and shots, being surrounded by old friends and new friends and anyone else who didn't want to be home for the festivities. Eventually I took to beginning my Christmas Day at Zeitgeist and then skateboarding all over San Francisco, dropping off small gifts and treats to bartenders who had to work the holiday—a few of the regulars got to calling me "Papa Noël." I wore a green, white, and red luchador mask under a Santa hat given to me by Cassy, a bartender at Zeitgeist, after I'd scared the shit out of her by bursting into the bar one rainy Christmas wearing the mask along with a black raincoat and black gloves with a black duffel bag slung over my shoulder. What I looked like was not the friendly spirit of Christmas. As I approached the bar, I saw the look of sheer terror on Cassy's face and halted.

"It's me!" I said. "It's Isaac! Sorry!"

Cassy slumped in relief, then shot me one of the more cutting glares I've ever deserved. "Jesus, Isaac, I almost hit the panic button!"

The gift giving was one day during the holidays, but there was a similar ethos about money circulating among those San Francisco bars year-round.

Money: Sometimes it's there; sometimes it's not. Sometimes it's handed to you, and sometimes you hand it to other people. Especially in the service industry. I soon became part of a large, drunk economy, going to other bars and restaurants and handing my money (plus generous tips) to bartenders, which they handed right back (plus generous tips) when they came to drink at Zeitgeist. Nobody was getting rich, but we could pay our bills—most of the time—and we could pay each other.

Like this: Every once in a while, Churchill, Elizabeth's baseball-loving partner—who also worked at the bar, and had taken me under his wing—would bring me to this old-school prime rib restaurant called the House of Prime Rib. Another San Francisco institution. We'd put on suits, drink a cold martini at Zeitgeist, and then take a taxi over to the steak-house. The reason for this ritual, Churchill had explained to me, was three-fold:

1) To remind ourselves why we did the job. We worked hard but made good money, which meant steaks.

2) To dress up and forget about the job. You work at a bar as busy as Zeitgeist (or any, really) you're gonna meet assholes, and what do assholes *love* to do? Make you feel less than, just for serving them. So the suit, the steaks, the night out—they're a reminder that we're human. We deserve.

3) To treat others like you want to be treated. It would always be a big night. Lots of booze, lots of laughter. And we made sure to extend our industry peers love and respect, which of course included leaving very large tips. We wanted to make some server or bartender's night, and share our own good fortune.

Churchill and Elizabeth didn't spend all their money, though. A lot of it they stuffed in a mattress in their sunny San Francisco apartment, right across the street from Zeitgeist, until they'd eventually saved up enough to buy a bar in Arizona. I keep meaning to visit.

AFTER A FEW years I moved on from working at the bar, and after a few more I moved on from San Francisco altogether. I held my goodbye party at Zeitgeist. As befitting a party thrown by me and for me, we drank during the day, all day.

If memory serves, I took a break in the middle of the party to go help a former roommate break into my old apartment on McCoppin Street (no crime—they'd locked themselves out). I had moved out of that place a few years back, had stopped working at the bar, and had stopped doing quite so many drugs, though I still drank.

And yet, through all the changes, Zeitgeist remained my home. To this day, no place feels more welcoming to me than when I cross through that big black door. It sounds cheesy, but it's a place where I know I belong. The place I feel most comfortable. Surrounded by friends and surrounded by strangers.

The bar no longer opens at nine A.M. every day. There are new refrigerators. Out back in the yard, there's a Jeremy Fish mural next to the pink elephants: a pink rabbit contorted into the shape of a skull, ears sticking out the top. The tow truck is now wrapped in protective chicken wire. Under the overpass down the block they've put in a skate park. The homeless encampment has grown.

Churchill is dead. The list of the dead could fill a paragraph. Steve is dead. Jef with one F is dead. I miss all of them. They're all up on the wall at Zeitgeist so I know where to go when I want to visit. Elizabeth is still running her bar in Arizona, a slice of the spirit of the Zeitgeist she knew over twenty years ago.

Todd still works there, though, and every time I see him he likes to remind me that he taught me everything I know. Many of the old heads are around, as are plenty of new ones, many of whom still live upstairs. A monastic life in their one-room rentals—party monks, dedicated to art and culture and bicycles and drinking and drugs and fun and love and sex and each other in a way so beautiful as to make you jealous—as if to make you weep.

This is most likely the part of the essay when I should say something about how I've stopped drinking. I haven't. I do drink less now than I did then, but it isn't out of some moralistic choice. My body's getting older. The hangovers last longer. And yes—I have found better ways to access my emotions than getting blotto on a Wednesday afternoon. When I first started (finally) going to therapy, after moving back to the East Coast, I made a habit of ducking into a nearby bar after every session. Eventually I told my therapist. She asked me that simple question, "Why?" and I explained how bars have always felt like home to me, especially one bar in particular. She asked again, "Why?" and I did my damnedest to explain everything that I've put into this essay. She looked at me, and did that frustrating thing that therapists so often do: She pointed out the obvious.

"Your home wasn't safe, it sounds like church wasn't safe, either. It's not surprising that you tried to find a place that was. To make something familiar. For you an unsafe space can feel comforting."

It's not like Zeitgeist fixed me. It just helped me heal a little. Every story I have is one step forward, two steps back. But I'm working on that. Now, anytime I visit San Francisco, it's still the first place I head to—before the hotel, before the friend's couch, before dropping off my bag or doing anything that could be construed as sensible. I get off the plane and from inside SFO, I can see the hills through the airport's wide windows, and I marvel at the California light, so different from the light on the East Coast. The light makes me suddenly and overwhelmingly lovestruck, the same way it did the first time I saw it back when I moved here (and now you know one of the other times I've experienced love at first sight in San Francisco, the moment I arrived). As I take the escalator down into the BART station, I'm mesmerized by the shifting, elusive shimmer of Ned Khan's *Wind Portal*, a giant art piece made up of more than two hundred thousand tiny, mirrored disks, and then I get on the train and ride until I reach Sixteenth and Mission. From there, I walk past all the eccentrics who still cling to those corners—the rough livers and the down-and-outs who'll be damned if new tech money shakes them out of their city before the next big earthquake comes to dislodge all these new monied folks driving up rent. San Francisco has always been a boom-and-bust town. It's another reason why I will always love it.

I stroll down Valencia. My bag is slung over my shoulder, heavy but feeling lighter the closer I get to my destination, and then I am there—I'm home. I walk through the big black door emblazoned with a skull and bunny ears, into the dark room I admired the first time I saw it fifteen years ago.

The last time I was at Zeitgeist, it was a Tuesday, and a couple had slipped into the photo booth, where they were—I am 100 percent certain—having sex. Some photos spilled out of the machine, and a woman who was working the door grabbed them and brought them over.

"What should we do?" The new-timer looked at me, which made sense. Once upon a time, I used to work there.

"Knock on the photo booth, tell 'em they gotta leave, and then let's all clap 'em out." And that's exactly what we did. The man skulked out holding his skateboard. The woman gave a giant curtsey and blew us all middle-finger kisses as she left, like she was the queen of fucking in this bar and fuck us all, her loyal subjects. Everyone will tell you that the time before the time you are at any given place is the best, but I am pretty sure this story incontrovertibly proves it: Zeitgeist still has the magic.

I'll usually tell myself that I'm only popping in for one, but soon enough I'll start catching up with the old familiar faces and making new friends. Rob's got a new tattoo of a beach with palm trees on the palm of his hand, and I want to wait until the light is right to take a photo. Next thing I know the light is gone and I'm wearing Rob's sweatshirt. Where did he go? At some point I'll remember the nights I used to sleep there but stop myself from following that line of thought, so I'll finally go check into my hotel, maybe stopping by Martuni's on the way. Knowing that I'll be back at Zeitgeist in the morning.

Because this is a story about loving the place that made you, even if it wasn't the place you were raised. And whether you're one-and-done or you're on a bender doing a wrap-around, you always come back to the ones you love.

Maybe I Could Die This Way

I remember the day I gave away my motorcycle. I awoke with a start that morning, not knowing where I was, then realizing I was in my own bedroom, then being relieved, then being overcome by a strange and inescapable wrongness. My mind felt both filthy and purified, heavy with hangover, all memories of the weekend wiped clean.

Step by step, I took the drunk's inventory and began looking around inside and all around myself. My body was warm and weighted down, still dressed in full leathers, but my hands were bare and folded on my stomach. I had laid myself out as deliberately as a body at a funeral. When I sat up, my leathers creaked, but nothing else did. I felt fine. Underneath me, the bed was still made, blankets and sheets neat as a pin.

I swung my body out of bed, springs squeaking too loudly in my small, orderly room. My helmet had been set down by the door, my gloves folded tidily beside it. Outside the window, I saw my motorcycle, gleaming in the San Francisco sun. Perfectly parked near the front of the building with not a scratch on it.

The last thing I remembered was drinking at a bar in Santa Cruz, over seventy miles away. I had decided that I was finally ready to take my bike out of the city, the longest ride I'd taken since I'd bought it. The drive down the coast had been transcendent. There is already no experience like driving the U.S. 101—especially if you're in a car with a roof that goes down—but if you're on a motorcycle? It's as close as I've ever gotten to touching the face of God, which is to say it's an experience that makes you say stuff like that. You fly, fly, fly down the road, enveloped in beauty, so close to it that you become a part of it.

By the time I had made it to Santa Cruz, I was weary. My ass hurt like hell, so I figured I should rest it on a barstool, deciding that I'd earned the right to, yet again, break the promise I'd made to myself when I first purchased this small-engined blue Honda from the eighties: No drinking and riding.

Thanks to my older friends, as a young kid in rural Massachusetts I learned how to drive long before I could get a license. We drove freely and recklessly and drank all the while, until one night I got into a car and noticed that the driver, who was high and drunk just like the rest of us, was wearing a neck brace, and suddenly I remembered that just a few months earlier the driver had been involved in a drinking-and-driving accident—as the driver—which had taken the lives of two of his passengers. His friends. As the car sped through the center of town I asked the driver to pull over and I got out.

For years I did my best to keep driving and drinking separate. I might have done dumb shit while drinking and dumb shit while driving, but never did the twain meet. It also helped that I never owned a car, mostly because I knew I might slip up, and I couldn't take the chance.

Conveniently, I also could never afford one.

But then I bought the motorcycle. What started off as a promise to never, ever drink while riding the bike quickly weakened into "A cold one beforehand every now and then isn't that bad," which then slipped into "It's okay to be drunk as long as I'm not going far."

I knew the ride to Santa Cruz was by any definition "going far." But, I reasoned, just because I went to a bar didn't mean I had to get drunk. So I found an unassuming dive and made that eternal promise to myself, the promise that has never once worked in the entire history of my lengthy drinking career, the promise that is all the more doomed the more fervently you have to make it: "I'll have just one."

One turned into two turned into making conversation with the bartender turned into "Why not stick around for a game of pool?" turned into making friends with the bartender turned into, finally, watching the sun set and the ocean breeze carry away the smoke from my bummed cigarette as I lit up in front of the bar, wondering if maybe I should rent a hotel room that I couldn't afford.

That had been my last memory before I woke up to find that I had somehow ridden all seventy miles back to San Francisco.

I took off my leathers, the hangover slamming my brain dully and rhythmically against my skull, my eyes strangely sandy and too swollen for their sockets. As I walked down the open stairwell of my building, the cool San Francisco air made me feel a tiny bit better for one deceptive, magnificent moment—until I was confronted with my bike. Not that anything was wrong with it, not even up close. It looked as though it had been parked using a ruler, and showed no signs of a fall. No dings or scrapes. Occasionally my spark plugs would be missing. This happens a lot with motorcycles, mostly because the porcelain makes breaking a car window a piece of cake. (Apparently you can also use them to smoke crack, but you can smoke crack with all kinds of things, and spark plugs break a car window so smoothly and easily that you'd think they were designed for that—if you didn't know they were spark plugs.) But even the spark plugs were intact.

Everything looked perfect. To understand that it wasn't, you had to know what I knew—about the broken promise, about riding all the way to Santa Cruz, about getting drunk at the bar, about using a brain and body that was so drunk it had stopped creating memories to ride a motorcycle seventy miles back to San Francisco. No, the perfection was ominous. It was a sign, a warning: a mobster visiting and showing you only the most kind and pleasant politeness, saying nothing of import, but chilling you almost senseless with the thought of what might happen should they find it necessary to visit you again.

I HAD BOUGHT the motorcycle off a guy who often drank at the bar I was still working at. He was a motorcycle mechanic but never joined a club, being one of those beautiful loners, hair slicked back in a kind of California cool that almost nobody can pull off unless they're up on a movie screen. He was older, maybe in his fifties, preternaturally youthful the way people who've never had kids (at least ones they know about) sometimes are.

When he sold me the bike, he gave me a card and said, "Call this person, they're good for insurance." Which was helpful. I'd never owned a vehicle before, and I was working three jobs and saving exactly zero dollars a month. If he hadn't prompted me, I would never have thought to get insurance.

I called the number and asked how much it would cost.

"You're in your twenties?" said the insurance man. "Probably around one hundred and twenty-five dollars."

"There's no way I can afford one hundred and twenty-five dollars a month," I said.

"This is your first bike, huh? It's not one hundred and twenty-five dollars a month. It's one hundred and twenty-five dollars a *year*."

"Oh," I said. That I could afford. But now it was sounding way too cheap, if anything. Suspiciously cheap. I wondered if my very cool motorcycle friend had maybe set me up with a dubious insurance person. "Can I ask why it's so, uh, affordable?"

The man exhaled. "Like I said, this is obviously your first bike. Kid, I like to shoot straight, and remember, I'm a rider myself, so this is the real and true answer: Insurance is so cheap because I most likely won't have to pay you out because when you crash you're most likely going to die."

"Oh," I said again. "Okay."

And I was. Okay with it. I remember very clearly thinking, "If I die while riding this extremely fun and well-built machine, I die, and that's okay." I had thought that, unlike a car, a motorcycle could hurt only me.

But now, standing in the street and staring at the very fast thing which had sped me home from one city to another without needing any assistance from my conscious mind, I recognized that as a lie. Other people drove on roads, and other people didn't know when you were fine with dying. I had been black-out drunk. I pictured a school bus full of kids swerving to avoid my bike, plummeting over the cliffs that the U.S. 101 hugs so tightly. Remembering that it had been a weekend night didn't make the image any easier to shake—I just substituted it for other vehicles, other kinds of terrified faces.

I hopped on the bike and took it around the corner to the bar. I handed the keys over to a tall blonde friend of mine, who—I was oddly relieved to hear—planned to sell the bike, since she could use the money even more than I could.

The rest of that day, and a few more after, I kept checking to see if there had been any accidents on the U.S. 101. None had been reported.

WHEN I WAS a kid, my mother made a couple of serious attempts on her own life, and talked about wanting to die so much that I got used to it. And when things at home got worse and worse, I started thinking about it too.

The first time I thought about killing myself I was maybe ten or twelve. I knew suicide was a sin, so I brought out all of my knives (our rural home was full of them) and pushed the blades through a wooden board so they stuck straight out the other side. I laid the board on the floor next to my bed, blade-side up. I had a history of rolling out of bed. Maybe I could die this way, without it being me who did it to myself.

For months I set the board up every night, but nothing ever happened.

Once, when I was twelve, my father took me to a memorial for a young man—one of his students—who had been found by his mother hanging from an extension cord in their garage. As the adults clustered around plates of microwaved hors d'oeuvres, the young people gathered in the boy's bedroom. There I found a knife, still jammed into the wall. My bedroom wall at the time had lots of knife marks too. They looked the same.

Undiagnosed mental illness runs in parts of my family on both sides. There's a heavily bearded great-granduncle in an old family photo of my mother's, who would disappear for weeks at a time, living in a small encampment in the woods and getting wasted on booze he made himself in a still. And though I have no real way of knowing this, except through the odd family rumor, take it from me: He wasn't getting drunk in the woods alone in a *happy* way.

My father's sister had been diagnosed with schizophrenia early on, and lived with her mother her entire adult life. Now her mother's dead. She still lives in her house, but she seems better, maybe even great. She's got a life, and I can honestly say that she's one of the happiest people I know. My father's brother wasn't so lucky—he died relatively young, after an isolated life full of ill health, both mental and physical. Decades later my father would send me the letter that his brother had sent him before he died, accusing their father of sexual abuse.

So many stories half told and half heard, so many grim intimations, so many obfuscating euphemisms. We were a classic New England family, incapable of discussing such things openly. Even when my mother, after another suicide attempt, was put on medication and kept briefly at a local hospital, we couldn't talk about it. She had been "sick," but once she came home she would be "better." Everything enveloped in a haze of mystery and shame. There was nothing I could do with the questions I had, the unmanageable anger and fear and nameless other feelings I was having. No place to put it all, so I kept it inside.

When you can't talk about something, you're prevented from naming and describing it, from making it real. And what you can't name and describe and make real becomes infinite and limitless and impossible to decipher or resolve because it can expand to fill your whole life and self to its tiniest corners or it can shrink to nothing; nothing being the size of things that are not real. You are alone—with it, with yourself. With this unsolvable problem.

THE MOTORCYCLE WAS gone but my feelings weren't. For a while I lived as I always had, drinking and doing drugs and going out, disguising stumbling as dancing. Most people saw me as a bouncing neon balloon, buoyant and carefree, while those who knew me better knew that I was recklessly pumping myself full of air, more and more, eager for the moment I'd pop into colorful tatters. Then become trash, then become nothing.

I remember a conversation where my ex, who wasn't my ex at the time, said to me, "If I died, you would be happy."

I was incredulous. "How can you say that?"

"You're looking for an excuse to drink yourself to death. That would give a reason to finish what you're so clearly starting."

This got to me. We began talking about ways that I could make a real change, get focused, distract myself, *anything*, and my ex brought up travel. "Did you ever do a semester abroad?"

I had not. I'd worked my way through college, so spending a semester or year in a foreign country where I couldn't make money hadn't been an option. Other than moving from the East Coast to the West, I had pretty much stayed put.

"There are ways. You could always teach English."

My parents were teachers, and they always seemed so unhappy. I had made a promise to myself, one of those ridiculous promises young people make to themselves when they know nothing of life but think they have it figured out. Promises like "I'm going to die by the age of twenty-seven," and "I'll never, ever teach." I didn't know what I wanted out of life, but after spending so much time staying late with my parents in the big, empty concrete squares where they worked, I knew I didn't want that.

"Well," my ex said, considering the options. "If you don't want to teach . . . there is this group . . ."

The Free Burma Rangers. FBR for short. I went and looked at the group's website. Studied it while sipping on a beer. I had already heard from my ex that FBR was a Christian organization, which made me a little wary, as I wasn't comfortable pushing Bibles or religion on people in need of substantive help.

But the website was reassuring. The Free Burma Rangers were a self-described "multi-ethnic humanitarian service movement working to bring help, hope and love to people in Burma." There was no talk of Christianity, only this: "Working in conjunction with local ethnic pro-democracy groups, FBR trains, supplies, and later coordinates with what becomes highly mobile multipurpose relief teams. After training, these teams provide critical emergency medical care, shelter, food, clothing and human rights documentation in their home regions."

"The idea is for them to get medical supplies to IDPs, internally displaced people," my ex explained.

"What does it mean, 'local ethnic pro-democracy groups'?"

"Rebels. Freedom fighters. Really depends on whose side you're on."

A bunch of indigenous tribes, including a group called the Karen (pronounced kah-REN, as opposed to the name of someone demanding to speak to your manager), had sided with the British during WWII, while the Burmese government had sided with the Japanese. When the Japanese were defeated, the British government didn't exactly stick around to make good on its promises to give the groups that fought with them their own countries. The Karen National Liberation Army, or the KNLA, had been fighting the Burmese government since 1949, along with numerous other groups.

Some called the country Myanmar and others Burma, since the regime changed the name to Myanmar in 1989. While the name Myanmar is more inclusive, many, including the United States, refused to recognize it, seeing as how the regime was a dictatorship.

As the FBR website puts it, "Over 70 years of civil war . . . have left Burma one of the poorest countries in the world. During this time, successive military dictatorships killed thousands of their own people and displaced millions in resistance areas. The resulting power vacuum has created a situation ripe for drug cultivation, child soldiers, acts of possible genocide, and starvation."

My ex said, "FBR smuggles medical supplies illegally over an international border into a conflict zone to assist in medical aid for IDPs who are being attacked by the Burmese junta."

"So like a drug smuggler, but in reverse." I didn't know much about Burma, but I did know that it was usually heroin being smuggled out, not medical supplies being smuggled in.

"Reverse isn't quite it, but yes." My ex added, "FBR also takes photos and videos to try and get attention from the media about what's going on in Burma. It's severely underreported. But I'm hoping to change that." My ex, who had worked with IDPs and taught English on the Thai–Burma border, would go on to become a brilliant investigative journalist and publish many articles and books about the ongoing conflict in Burma, all of which are much more comprehensive and better reported than what you'll find here.

I went home and did more research online. I learned that the founder of FBR was a man named David Eubank. The son of missionaries, Eubank had grown up in Thailand. He was a pastor and ex–Green Beret member of the U.S. Special Forces, who returned to Southeast Asia in the late nineties and saw the escalation of Burmese military activity against the Karen people. Villages were destroyed, many people were killed, and according to the FBR website, "more than 100,000 people were forced from their homes in a program of violence which was designed to remove people from land in order to make way for developing business interests."

Eubank started an initiative called the Global Day of Prayer for Burma, but wanted to do more, and began going into Burma to bring aid and relief to the oppressed ethnic minorities under attack by the Burmese government.

Though FBR was a Christian organization, and the Karen had been converted to Christianity by extremely well-armed British colonizers, the website said that FBR didn't proselytize, and they helped anyone who needed help, not just Christians. Groups like the Karenni, the Chin, the Shan, and many others. During my childhood years in the Catholic Worker homeless shelter, I'd seen the good that religious organizations could do for those in need. So why not try to give back? As long as I wasn't handing out Bibles.

I decided to go. As this was before GoFundMe or Kickstarter, I set up a fundraising party at a bar, sort of like we used to do in the town where I'd grown up in Massachusetts. When a family's house burned down or someone's dad died, a tin coffee can would go up at the local gas station or small grocery store with a sign reading, simply, HELP. Help was what I needed; also, help was what I needed to be able to give in order to feel anything other than this inward-looking grayness. It'd been a minute since I'd actually helped anyone, done any work to clearly and unambiguously contribute to someone's well-being. It had been a minute since I'd actually been of use.

ARRIVING IN CHIANG Mai, I was exhausted. I'd never spent that much time on a plane. It seemed impossible that you could be in the air for so long. It felt like I had *moved* into the plane, me and a hundred roommates in a shitty studio apartment in the sky.

San Francisco to Tokyo, Tokyo to Bangkok, Bangkok to Chiang Mai. The largest city in northern Thailand, Chiang Mai is 435 miles north and just a smidge to the east of Bangkok, the country's capital.

I stumbled off the airplane, jetlagged and not sure where to go. Despite my vow to learn some of the language before I'd left, I knew little more than "please" and "thank you" and, most importantly, "sorry."

Fortunately an FBR member was there to scoop me up, escorting me outside the airport where we found a songthaew, which was a truck with two benches and a covering that served as a cab alongside Chiang Mai's, well, cabs, and also Thailand's famous tuk tuks. The team member told the driver where to go and I immediately collapsed into the back, lying down on one of the benches and kicking up my feet to take one of those jet-laggy naps that feels less like real restorative sleep and more like getting your mind and senses partially switched off.

"I wouldn't do that if I were you," the FBR volunteer said. I cracked open one eye. "What? Sleep?"

"No. I mean I wouldn't put your feet up."

I sat up and set my feet back down onto the bed of the truck. "Why's that?"

"Listen. In Thailand, pointing your feet, especially the soles of your feet, at anyone is considered extremely rude. You're basically flipping off every single person we drive by and everyone behind us."

"Shit. Sorry. I didn't know."

He wasn't done with me yet. "Those your only shoes?" he said, eyeing the heavy cowboy boots I was wearing.

"Uh . . . Yeah."

"You're gonna need new ones. You know, because it gets hot here?"

THE FBR MEMBER told me I'd be staying at a storehouse where the team stowed all their supplies before packing them up into rice bags and smuggling them over the Thai–Burma border. But before I got to collapse onto whatever kind of sleeping area I'd have in the storehouse, we went to dinner at a volunteer's home.

I got instant whiplash. I'd just gotten to Thailand, and now I was walking into this house that felt like a portal back to the United States. The spaghetti dinner, which was held every Thursday, was full of other FBR members and their families—all white, all Christian, all volunteers. The older ones were doctors and a few of the younger ones were the doctors' kids. Some had been with FBR for years, a few were new arrivals like myself. One family had been working at a hospital in Pakistan before they came to Chiang Mai.

Most of the central FBR figures, including founder Dave Eubank, weren't at dinner that night. They were in Burma, or "in country," and would be for months.

"Are you Christian?" one of the grandmothers asked as she filled my plate.

"Uh, I was raised Catholic."
She smiled. "Close enough."

THE STOREHOUSE WAS near Chiang Mai University and was filled with empty rice sacks and packing materials and piles of donated clothes and medical supplies stacked on top of each other. I slept on a bedroll in the corner and showered using a plastic bucket and a small showerhead that, despite the heating attachment, only ran cold. I brushed my teeth with bottled water, while examining the whiteboard that was covered with packing lists and Bible verses. I read bits of Paul the Apostle's letter to the Ephesians:

> *Finally, my brethren, be strong in the Lord, and in the power of his might.*
>
> *Put on the whole armor of God, that ye may be able to stand against the wiles of the devil. For we wrestle not against flesh and blood, but against principalities, against powers, against the rulers of the darkness of this world, against spiritual wickedness in high places. Above all, taking the shield of faith, wherewith ye shall be able to quench all the fiery darts of the wicked. And take the helmet of salvation, and the sword of the Spirit, which is the word of God . . .*

MY FIRST WEEK at FBR wasn't all that different from my stint working on a congressional campaign in Pennsylvania, just with a hotter climate and much better food. The headquarters were located on the other side of the Old City, not too far from the storehouse, in a building that housed two groups.

Officially, the building was the home of Partners Relief & Development, a Christian NGO that "through holistic action demonstrates God's love to children and communities made vulnerable by war and oppression." Steve Gumaer, the founder, lived in Chiang Mai with his Norwegian family and would have me over for dinner often, where his daughters would entertain everyone by making fun of my tattoos. While celebrating New Year's Eve at his house, Steve taught me how to make a floating lantern, and I watched the sky fill up with what could only be described as the largest, most beautiful and soulful collective fire hazard that I have ever seen.

For the most part, Partners' offices looked like that of any other nonprofit, full of cubicles and printers that were always running out of ink, bustling with volunteers and a few paid employees. An older retired couple who had come over to help out for a few months eventually ended up moving to Thailand permanently, dedicating the rest of their lives to the cause.

On my first day in the office, I was given a familiar task. I stuffed envelope after envelope for a mailer. Although this time it wasn't to get a person elected to Congress, but to publicize the upcoming FBR Global Day of Prayer for Burma.

"Are you a Christian?" one of my fellow envelope-stuffers asked.

"Raised Catholic," I said.

"Good enough."

It was the third floor, though, that distinguished Partners Relief & Development from other nonprofits. Wallpapered in maps, the third floor was full of green military bags and walkie-talkies. I looked down to see a stack of satellite phones by my feet. Everyone was dressed in green—military pants with cargo pockets and tight ranger-green T-shirts that had FBR printed in small letters on the chest and this message on the back:

LOVE EACH OTHER.

UNITE AND WORK FOR FREEDOM, JUSTICE, AND PEACE.

FORGIVE AND DON'T HATE EACH OTHER.

PRAY WITH FAITH, ACT WITH COURAGE, NEVER SURRENDER.

The FBR team member showing me around grinned and said, "Wanna see something?" before darting around the room and making all the maps disappear with dizzying speed. Wall maps rolled upward with one quick jerk or were obscured by unfurling banners and flags, while those spread out on the table were rolled up or covered over by presumably more innocent-looking pieces of paper. It was like a magic trick.

"Just in case the place has an unexpected visitor," he said. I asked if that had ever happened.

"Not yet," he responded. "But you never know."

It was starting to sink in—for real—that the nonprofit organization I'd signed up to work for was also, perhaps, a super illegal one.

EACH DAY I'D go into the office, where I edited spreadsheets with updated donor addresses and kept an eye on the FBR inbox for emails from potential volunteers. I'd tell everyone what they wanted to know, which hopefully persuaded those who already didn't seem like a good fit not to come. Once in a while I'd help write grant requests.

Whatever my specific tasks, my day at the office always started the same way. I'd kick off my cowboy boots outside the front door, where they loomed among a sea of flip-flops, their worn leather slouching awkwardly like the kids who had hit their growth spurt earlier than the rest of the class. I kept wearing the boots, just like I kept wearing pants, despite the heat, despite the Thai workers often making fun of my senseless commitment to keeping myself covered up.

IN MY OFF-HOURS, I'd wake up with the roosters who lived in the empty lot near the storehouse and go for a jog past the Chiang Mai Zoo, exploring the windy, lush trails and cascading waterfalls I'd found nearby. Or I'd hang out at the storehouse and clean up the place. As wild dogs—furless and tiny, cute yet somehow intimidating—roamed the small street, I would sweep the stoop and pull up any weeds growing from between cracks in the concrete. Neighbors noticed my efforts and started waving at me.

Every morning I bought meat and rice from a woman who worked a cart at the end of my block. I'd get a coffee, too, which was always sweet and pale with condensed milk. At first I had made futile efforts to order it black, but then gave up.

At night, the whiteboard with the packing lists and Bible verses would be illuminated by the DVDs playing on my laptop: plastic-wrapped bootlegs I'd buy from the night market. It was always a gamble whether the movie would be dubbed over in Chinese. I'd watch them either way, to pass the time. Or I'd spend hours writing emails to friends at home, who would usually respond by wondering what I was doing there in the first place.

AFTER I'D SPENT enough time doing office work and not screwing it up too badly, FBR began trusting me with other kinds of tasks. My job became filling the empty rice sacks with medical supplies, gauze, mosquito nets, donated clothes, and other items, then sewing them closed with a large needle and strips of plastic. We'd load the bags up onto a big, white diesel-engine truck owned by the group, which would be driven to the Thai–Burma border, where they would then be smuggled to internally displaced people on the other side.

One day Rebecca, who pretty much ran the show in Chiang Mai, logistics-wise, asked if I could do her a favor. Early on she had taught me a lot of the basics—things like how to use international prepaid phone cards and send and receive mail from back home.

"Listen, we wouldn't ask you to do this, but everybody is in country for the most part right now. And, well, we can trust you, yeah?"

My response was immediate. "Of course! What do you need?"

I had no idea what I was about to be asked to do, but I was sick of doing office work.

Rebecca handed me a debit card. "I need you to go to the bank . . ." she began.

Now, I don't remember the exact amount of money that Rebecca told me to withdraw from the bank. What I do remember is how the bank teller had needed to use a machine to count out the stacks, which he wrapped with currency straps before handing them over to me. I had never seen, much less held, this much money in U.S. dollars, and since this was in Thai baht, there was a lot more of it.

I remember the weight of the money. How heavy my bag was. When I got on the scooter that I'd recently rented to help me get around town, I wondered for a moment if all the extra weight would tip me over. The second part of the task I'd been given was to take the money and drop it off at various places, mostly banks, but also to one old woman who would be using the money to buy supplies to smuggle into Burma.

Most clearly of all, I remember what it felt like to drive that money around Chiang Mai.

And when I say "clearly" I mean that I can access this memory whenever I want. It is always close at hand. I wouldn't be surprised if, when I die, this memory makes it into the Top Ten Moments from Your Life Memory Slideshow™ that your brain sees right as it starts to spark and blink out.

In this memory, I am driving my newly rented scooter around a roundabout. The sun is shining so bright and hot that it makes the money-filled bag on my back feel all the heavier.

I am shocked by the sight, the feel, the fact of so much money, and for the briefest of moments I entertain the idea of absconding with the cash and starting a new life somewhere in the Northern Thai countryside—but I don't really mean it, even to myself. It's just a brief flash, the vision of a totally fresh start made possible by something I would never do. Because more than anything else, I am happy. I am so, so happy in all the different ways I like to be happy but that don't usually all match up and click into place like this, which is to say: Here I am, zooming around on a scooter with a bag full of cash, feeling illicit and independent and free, while at the same time doing something of purpose. Something *good*. This, perhaps, is the first time in a long while that I don't feel like dying.

SOON I WAS doing more of these money drops, as well as picking up supplies and buying satellite phones and other expensive equipment. Then came the day Rebecca asked me, "You have a license, right?"

The truck was big. Its exhaust pipe snaked up and over the cab. When I'd first asked Rebecca about its use, she had responded simply, "Like a snorkel. To drive through rivers." To get behind the wheel, I had to swing myself up into the driver's seat. In the back were piles of rice sacks filled with medical supplies and other important gear, stacked so high they spilled over the sides of the bed of the truck, and were held in place only by a stretchy web of mesh made out of bungee cords. Seeing out the back would be impossible. I tried not to think about it.

Rebecca was quizzing me. "And what do you say if you get pulled over at a checkpoint?"

"These supplies are for schools and refugee camps on *this* side of the border," I said. "And I'm either a preacher or a teacher."

The concept had been repeated to me many times over. Preacher or a teacher. Preacher or a teacher. Preacher or a teacher.

"Right, but you have to pick *one* of those. In your case, I'd go with teacher. But yeah, that's basically it. Just follow the directions and our people will be there to meet you."

And so I went. I did this job a bunch of times, driving the truck toward Mae Sot or Mae Hong Son, or other spots along the Thai–Burma border, often going through Namtok Mae Surin National Park. Though I drove through roadblocks, never once was I stopped. Always waved through—I never had to decide whether to be a teacher or a preacher.

The specifics might change, but overall the drive stayed the same. I traveled on regular paved roads for miles and miles, hours and hours, toward the border, and somewhere—at a nebulous point that felt like it was right by the border—I took a right or left off the paved road onto a logging road, where I drove until I was met by a group of people, which usually included members of the Karen and other indigenous groups, as well as FBR medics and the occasional white person. Everyone would strap the supplies onto their backs or heads or, sometimes, load them onto a donkey, ready to ferry across a river or through the jungle.

Google Maps was in its infancy then, and not particularly trustworthy, especially when you got off main roads. So it was just me, the truck, the supplies, and a printout of directions from Rebecca, sometimes scrawled with notes like, "If you pass a gas station, you've gone too far." I got lost a couple of times, but never for too long, thankfully, because the last thing I wanted to do was make an embarrassing phone call to Rebecca to plead for help just because I hadn't made the time to learn Thai before coming here and couldn't ask anyone else; but then again, what would I have said if I had known Thai? "Can you please direct me to the spot where I'm supposed to meet some folks so we can break international law?"

After a couple weeks of this, Rebecca gave me another job. "Need you to go to the border."

"Another drop?"

"Actually, no. A pickup this time. We've got some FBR team members who are coming out."

ONE OF THE pickups I did was of an ex–U.S. Army Ranger whom Rebecca would later marry. On our ride back to Chiang Mai, he told me about how he spent half the year working geology jobs around the globe and the other half volunteering with the FBR. "It feels good to help people. Wouldn't you agree?"

I did, and I remember being a bit fascinated by this tall, wiry man who spent his free time running around the jungles of Southeast Asia.

Sometimes pickups of team members coming out were combined with drop-offs of team members going in. I don't remember if I picked up the Frenchman alone or not—he might have come out with the geologist/ex-Ranger but slept in the back of the truck during the ride home. In any case, what I do remember is being back in Chiang Mai, and the Frenchman saying, "Let's go out!"

I suggested my favorite bar—a rock-and-roll joint close to the storehouse owned by two sisters who appreciated that I let the local students practice their English on me and also that I tipped—but he cut me off. "No. Not to some bar. I mean *out.* To a club. Let's get a bottle," he said, his accent sounding triply, quadruply French.

Though I've never liked going out to clubs, I figured I should let the guy have the night he wanted. He had just gotten back to Chiang Mai, after all. So I agreed.

The club was mostly empty, techno booming all the louder as if to compensate for the absence of people. We sat on low black plastic couches. We weren't dressed well—we simply didn't have the clothes—but it didn't matter, because we had the money to get a bottle of Johnnie Walker. (By the way, I would love to know the promotional budget for Johnnie Walker in Thailand, because that shit is *everywhere*, like brush-your-teeth-with-it-instead-of-water everywhere.) The bottle arrived quickly with a bucket of ice and we began working our way through it.

The Frenchman said something, blanketed by techno. I asked him to repeat himself. "I think this is one of the last great adventures on the planet," he yelled. "You join the army, it's basically sitting around and waiting. Often you never get to see combat."

I had friends in the military who'd disagree—who saw more than enough combat in Iraq and Afghanistan to know that it was not at all something to be desired—but I kept my mouth shut and let him continue.

"But here, you sign up, they make sure you're okay, and bam! You're in country. This is real danger. These are real risks. And you're absolutely on the right side of history. Maybe it's like this in the Legionnaires. But no, I think this is it. The last great adventure. How lucky we are to have found it."

I asked him what he did inside.

"I take pictures. I love the filming, the photographs. It all feels so clandestine. I'm telling you, when I was in there we were taking photos of the army and, Jesus, listen, we were right next to them. There's no other word to describe it but thrilling. This is the kind of stuff Hemingway wrote about, fighting fascists in Spain. And we're doing it."

At the time I remember laughing with him, even though I felt vaguely queasy and turned off by what he was saying—the over-the-top macho posturing, the Hemingway comparisons, something else I didn't yet have the humility and understanding to examine too closely. Looking back now, I can see so clearly what the issue was: We were two white dudes who had come to Southeast Asia from countries that had notably fucked things up in Southeast Asia, talking about a devastating civil war that had left so many dead and displaced like it was our own personal adventure.

"Do you think you'll go back?" I asked.

"How can one walk away from the last great adventure left?" He smiled. "Come on, let's hit another place."

I politely turned him down, and he went off into the night while I turned around and went back to my bedroll in the storehouse. Christians, ex-military, adventure junkies—FBR attracted all types. And then there was me, a barback who didn't know what to do with his life, much less if it was worth living.

THE FIRST TIME I went in country, I had no advance warning. I had simply thought we were heading up to the border and staying there for a few days. And even that prospect was so exciting that I couldn't sleep the night before—knowing that the next night I'd be far from the cities, out under the stars.

The truck would take us past Mae Sariang to the Salween River. The group included Dr. Bob, an evangelical eye doctor from Anchorage, plus his son, along with a few other FBR members and volunteers.

We stopped for a bite in Mae Sariang and continued to the Salween. The moment I found out that I was going into Burma was the opposite of momentous: At some point, I asked someone if we were going in country and they gave me the "Yes, dumbass" look.

At the banks of the river, we were met by Peter, a round, short Karen man whose bright blue knit pom-pom hat had my cowboy boots beat in the wrong-for-the-weather sweepstakes. As we unloaded our stuff, Dr. Bob initiated another quick prayer, which he'd already done twice on this trip so far. Still, I went with it. After all, he was the VIP. We were bringing Dr. Bob in to give eye exams to the IDPs.

Below where we parked the trucks, a handful of long, skinny riverboats quietly clicked against one another while waiting for passengers. We walked down. Our boat was driven by a young Karen man around my age who was smoking a cigarette. His T-shirt said ROCK NOT DIE.

The boat ride was an hour. Some slept, while others took photos of the shoreline and people we passed. Peter, who was the head of the IDP camp we were visiting, spoke English, so I sat at the front of the boat and talked with him.

Ei Tu Hta had more than four thousand IDPs in its main camp, and recently had to start another camp about fifteen minutes farther up the river for another two thousand people. The camp had been there for two years, formed with the tacit permission of the Thai government, who had an impromptu army outpost directly across the river. Ei Tu Hta was now surrounded on three sides by the Burmese Army. Their backs were against the Salween. But there hadn't been any attacks yet, and Peter thought that because the camp got so much attention from the Thai, it would be safe for the time being.

"That is where the Burmese soldiers live." He pointed to a large two-story hut built from thatched wood, with a roof made out of leaves.

"A Burma base?" I asked.

"Yes," he said, and laughed. "Our neighbors."

When we arrived at the camp, no one was around. It almost seemed abandoned. I trudged along, carrying the eye doctor's equipment in a heavy, orange plastic suitcase, and caught up to Peter walking ahead.

"Where is everyone?" I asked.

He pointed as we rounded a corner. The camp was split by a shallow but wide stream. On one side were more thatch and bamboo houses, but on the other side the thick jungle abruptly fell away to reveal a big, open dirt field.

There in the field was a gathering of a couple hundred people watching a soccer game. The players wore uniforms, which Peter told me had been recently donated. The camp had twenty-two teams and played year-round.

Across the stream Peter brought us to the house where we'd be staying. I kicked off my boots and climbed the wooden ladder, rungs worn smooth. In the house, I saw that the bamboo poles ran only every few feet, and the rest of the floor was just thatched wood. I started worrying about falling through the floor, about how it would be a dumb end to my dumb life—which, now that I was somewhere else doing some specific things for some specific people who needed it, I reflexively tried to keep—as I worked to hide the fact that I was awkwardly jumping from one secure bamboo pole to another while setting up my mosquito net. An FBR member noticed and told me that I could be three times as heavy and still wouldn't even come close to falling through the thatching. "So quit hopping around."

A few houses down was the clinic. It was a house identical to all the others, distinguished only by some writing in blue chalk on the outside. We set up Dr. Bob, and soon he was ready to see patients.

There was only one problem: How were we going to get kids to stop in for eye exams, when there was a *fantastically* exciting soccer game going on at the same time? It didn't help that the out of bounds line on the left edge of the field skirted the creek, and every so often an overzealous player would fall ten feet into the water below.

Half an hour had gone by with nobody showing up. Dr. Bob grew tense, pacing around the clinic, fretting about the prospect of having raised all this money and put in all this effort to come all this way and *not* being able to do his good deed. I told him to hold on, that I would go find some kids, and climbed down the ladder.

Though Dr. Bob had brought a bag of toys to amuse the kids while they were waiting, it was clear that these toys weren't shit. (No offense, Dr. Bob.) I didn't see how a bunch of yellow plastic finger puppets with somewhat creepy smiles was going to compete with a big game of soccer/*Wipeout*. But I was good with kids, and I felt confident that I could bring them over. A little language barrier, I reasoned, had nothing on the power of funny faces and goofing around.

This proved . . . inaccurate. After balancing my way over the creek by sliding across a fallen tree, I walked around the soccer crowd for a while. Everyone was courteous, offering smiles and brief greetings, but then would quickly turn their attention back to the game. Me making goofy faces and pointing at the clinic couldn't hold a candle to the sight of soccer players flying through the air and splashing thunderously into the creek.

Because—I said it once and I'll say it again—what a game it was! The guys on the field, in contrast to the chill and kind demeanors of the nonplayers, were combining swerves and feints and fancy footwork with straight-up body slams. At one point, when I had finally captured the attention of a little kid with a game of peekaboo, the crowd gasped, and the kid looked away. So did I, to be honest. Another player had slid right off the field and plummeted into the creek.

I was about to give up, go back to Dr. Bob and admit defeat, when I noticed a little girl in a green dress. Her face had been painted with three light brown circles, a custom of the Burmese hill tribes. She looked up at me and shot an enormous jet of red betelnut spit in my direction.

Although I hadn't taken any pictures of people up to now, not wanting to do so without permission and cause offence, I took one of her, and immediately turned the camera around to show her the photo. She beamed. I took more, showing her the photos as other kids became curious and demanded that I take their photos too.

I marched back across the fallen tree with a line of kids in tow. Many of them didn't even bother with the tree—they just stamped their way straight through the creek. I planted myself outside the clinic like a carnival barker, except instead of shouting I was miming, and instead of urging people to go inside the big top, I was convincing them to wait in line to get their eyes checked.

For more than two hours the children sat around wearing yellow disposable eyepatches over first one eye and then the other, and, using a board set up in front of them, pointed to the symbols that matched a rotating board ten feet away. Those who passed were given one of the aforementioned creepy yellow finger puppets, while those who didn't had their eyes examined more closely by Dr. Bob. Lots of them left with glasses.

All the while, the pressure was on me to keep up the enter-tainment. The take-a-photo, show-a-photo gambit was wearing thin, and some of the kids were starting to drift toward the soccer field again.

I thought fast, remembered the time that a clown visited my elementary school and taught us how to juggle. Clearly now was the time to bring that skill I had never used since out again.

With the crowd's eyes on me, I picked up three rocks and dove right in.

Over the course of maybe five minutes, I managed to catch what I tossed about three times. And no—not three, or even two times in a row. Instead of showing the kids a display of the skill and dexterity it took to keep three objects cycling through the air, I was showing them how hilarious it was to pick up rocks, hurl them toward the sky, and then let them fall on top of me. They, of course, followed suit.

I tried desperately to mime a non-murdery "stop it" (aka not the neck slice) as the kids laughed and yelped at the falling rocks. Dr. Bob and the other FBR members testing the kids gave me the side-eye, so then, out of pure desperation, I grabbed one of the creepy yellow finger puppets and put it on my thumb. The kids dropped their rocks and raised their finger puppets, watching expectantly, and maybe a little dubiously, like, "Okay, guy, we've already played with these things and they're pretty boring, but show us what you got."

I waggled my thumb. The puppet stayed boring. Then, in an inspired and completely accidental move I grabbed the bottom of the puppet and snapped it off my thumb so quickly that it turned inside out, emitting an odd, hollow *pop!*

A hundred *pops!* immediately followed, and then continued into the evening. Even though with each new *pop!* I'm sure the other adults cursed my name to the heavens, this was luckily counterbalanced by the fact that the kids stayed amused until the sun went down and Dr. Bob had finished giving eye exams for the day.

AT NIGHT, THE moon was enormous and the jungle quiet. A woman by a fire sold small tangerines for a baht, and a man with no teeth gave us a strong, hot beverage for free. For the first time all day we weren't followed by children, as they were watching Bible stories projected onto a small, tattered screen. The sound was blasted through loudspeakers to compensate for the *whoosh* of the generator that powered the projector. Other than the fire and the Bible stories and the moon, there was no light at all. That was enough, though, for me to see that the camp was indeed protected. I spotted four Karen men with M16s slung against their backs, walking in meandering circles around the outskirts of the camp.

Back at the house, I stretched out on a handwoven mat and read by candlelight under dusty blankets. As I drifted off, the Bible cartoons were replaced by poorly dubbed eighties action movies.

The next day I woke early. I strolled around the camp and eventually sat down on a log as the sun rose above the make-shift soccer field. A young man sat down next to me. He was sixteen or seventeen years old at most, and I recognized him, from the day before, when he'd been one of the many folks laughing at my antics with the children.

We started chatting, and I asked him, "What do you want to do when you get out of here?" Immediately I regretted my question, which I'd posed as if the *here* were some small Massachusetts town he could just drive away from.

But the young man only smiled. "I want to go to your country. I want to ski."

"Ski?" I asked, certain I'd misheard him.

"Yes. Ski. Downhill. Have you ever?"

"I have." Then, caught off guard again, I asked, "Have you?"

He laughed. "Of course not!" He looked out over the field. "What's it like?"

And that is when I undertook the harder-than-it-seems task of describing snow. Which he had of course seen in movies, and heard about, but, you know . . .

We kept talking. A lot of our conversation had this general format: He'd ask me something about the United States, and I'd tell him.

"The U.S. is awesome," he would conclude.

"Karen State is awesome too," I would say.

"I want to go to the U.S.," he would respond.

And then I'd say, "I want to spend more time in Karen State." He would look at me as if I was delusional and then we would both laugh uproariously, sometimes because it was funny and other times because we were nervous and didn't know what to say. Sometimes both. We talked about baseball, basketball, soccer, and hamburgers. He told me about farming, different animals and birds, his family, and why he had chosen not to fight with the KNLA.

"I am angry, but my family is still alive and I want to provide for them. I have become a good English speaker. I want to be a teacher."

I admired that. I couldn't do anything to make his life easier or better, but I wanted to do something, anything. I couldn't even give advice without being naive, hypocritical, wrong. So I just handed him my aviator sunglasses, which I'd noticed him looking at every so often. It felt like a useless gesture to me, but he was stoked by this unexpected gift, and thanked me profusely. We said our goodbyes and he immediately ran toward the heart of the camp.

That second day, word had spread and adults and children lined up to test their eyes and get general checkups. Dr. Bob was an eye-examining machine, and despite his tendency to stop and pray at (what seemed to me) random intervals, he was good at what he did. We worked straight through lunch.

The children were no longer intimidated by me, and what had previously been a performer-audience relationship now became an interactive experience. They were constantly surrounding me, climbing on me, hugging me with all their might.

I'd never known so many smiles. More than once I found myself forgetting that these children had been forced from their homes by soldiers who hunted their people relentlessly; that they now lived in deep poverty wedged between enemy military camps and a large river, on the other side of which was a nonresponsive country that did not want them. What a luxury to forget.

Late in the afternoon, our boat arrived and we had to leave. Dr. Bob had just finished seeing his last patient. We had conducted numerous general health checkups, given out over fifty pairs of reading glasses, and filled over sixty prescriptions. Next month the prescription glasses would be delivered, along with one hundred more pairs of reading glasses. I felt like we'd just thrown a pebble at a mountain in an attempt to move it.

But as we walked down the steep sandy banks to our boat, it was hard to ignore the joy all around me. Halfway down the bank I fell in the sand and was immediately covered in laughing children. The girl in the green dress from the day before led the rest of the group in a giant tackle, and trapped at the bottom, I burst into laughter.

A hand reached through and helped me to my feet. My old aviator sunglasses reflected me back at myself. The teenage boy I'd been talking with earlier handed me a plastic necklace with the image of a tiny flag hand-painted on it.

"The Karen State flag. I made this for you. You will come back."

The paint looked fresh. I wanted to tell him that the sunglasses looked great on him, but I was overwhelmed. "Ta bluh doh mah," I said simply. "Thank you very much," in Karen. The only phrase in his language I had mastered. I thanked him for his kindness again in English and made a promise to myself to bring back an equally thoughtful gift the next time I came to Ei Tu Hta.

The boat pulled away from the shore. A throng of well-wishers jumped and waved. We drove down the river, baking in the sun. Dr. Bob was smiling as big as the children. He prayed again, but I was no longer mentally rolling my eyes at his fervid Christianity. He had done something for this group of people. Something tangible and good. Peter tapped my shoulder. We were both at the head of the boat again. "Soldiers," he said, pointing downriver.

I didn't know how I'd overlooked them: three men, up to their waists in the water, shirts off, washing themselves and their uniforms. Above them was the base we passed a few days before. A surge of anger shot through me. I wanted to swim toward them and scream at them.

"They are children," Peter said, as if reading my mind. "No choice. They are brainwashed to hate."

Now I wanted to plead with the soldiers. I wanted to show them pictures of all the children I'd met, try to reason with them, to explain that these people meant them no harm. I wanted to take them to Ei Tu Hta for a soccer game. I wanted to find the language to say all of these things, the language to argue back.

The sun hung low in the sky as they watched us go by. One soldier put up his hand.

I didn't wave back.

THE SECOND TIME I went in country, it was to Shan State.

Sharing a border with China, Laos, and Thailand, Shan State is home to many ethnic groups and their armies. It's also an area where a *lot* of drugs are made. Originally heroin, but now fentanyl and methamphetamine—crystal, plus the little red Yaba pills found in so many of the nearby refugee camps.

The roads we drove in on were treacherous. Cinematic roads: the kinds that up until that point I had seen only in movies. Dirt slid down steep cliffs as our jeeps plunged through the jungle, the drivers knowing no other way but forward. Eventually we got as far as the roads went, and exited the vehicles, strapping bags onto our backs.

"Let's gather for a prayer," someone said.

We all made a circle. I'd grown accustomed to bowing my head quietly as a prayer was said.

"Isaac, do you care to lead the prayer?"

My head whipped up. I stuttered inconclusively.

"We know," an FBR member said with a smile. "You were raised Catholic. Give it a shot."

I said a prayer off the top of my head, and whatever it was passed muster. With that, we hiked through the forest, up and down muddy ravines. We watched out for landmines—which I had been warned about, but still wasn't quite sure how to avoid, except by placing my feet cautiously.

Eventually we were met by men in uniforms driving trucks, who brought us to what could be described only as a town/military base. Right away, I could tell that the Shan were very different from the Karen: One of the soldiers offered me a gun to carry; they had plenty. I chose to decline.

The Karen lived in the jungles, armed with rifles that looked like they'd been left behind by the British after WWII. Their homes, made of leaves and wood, were raised high up on poles. The Shan lived in a compound where some of the buildings were concrete, and modern weapons and uniforms were everywhere. Soldiers were numerous, often outnumbering the civilians. The Karen's houses melded with their natural environment, their camp cobbled together through ingenuity and a lack of resources; whereas the Shan compound showed that they were a rebellion with financing.

My feelings clashed—the Karen camp had seemed safer, with its games and its laughing children and its movie nights. The only guns I'd seen there had been glimpsed momentarily, at the outskirts of camp. With the Shan, everywhere you looked there were guns—weaponry and uniforms and serious, hard faces. Which could be intimidating until you remembered that it was the Karen camp that was truly defenseless, that could be razed at a moment's notice. Everything that made the Shan compound feel so dangerous, so close to the edge of a skirmish or battle, was in fact what made it far more safe.

The Shan gave us special treatment. Though the Karen had offered us what food they had, the Shan had the means to throw a dinner in our honor. After the meal, one of the officers offered me a drink and I sat, enjoying the alcohol that I never in a million years would have expected to receive on this journey.

"So, where do you come from?"

"San Francisco. California, in the United States."

"And what do you do?"

"I, uh, I wash glasses at a bar."

The officer laughed and nodded. "A dishwasher?"

"Yeah."

The officer laughed again. "Or," he offered, "you're CIA."

I don't remember how I got out of that one, though the officer didn't seem to be bothered at all either way. Later I told another FBR team member, a buff dude with a goatee, about the fact that a Shan officer had implied that we were CIA.

"Yeah, we get that a lot."

"But . . . we're not, right?" I said.

"Isaac," he said. "You used to wash dishes. I'm a Christian from Oregon. We ain't CIA."

I was a hit with the Shan soldiers, mainly because of my tattoos. At this point I was getting used to communicating through means other than spoken language, and with the Shan soldiers we could bond over their many, *many* tattoos. There's a photo of me posing with one such soldier, the bear skull inked onto my forearm side by side with the tiger's face on the back of his hand. We are both around the same age, same wild grins across our faces.

In the evening I slept in a hammock I'd brought with me, tied between the front ends of two trucks parked outside the buildings where the other FBR members stayed. I slept in my clothes, now the same de facto uniform the others wore: cargo pants and a dark-green FBR T-shirt.

A Shan soldier who spoke English came by. "Be careful of the tiger," he said.

"The *what* now?"

"Oh, yes," he said breezily, walking away. "There is a tiger in the jungle."

I was never able to confirm if there was actually a tiger or if that soldier was just fucking with me. Most likely the latter. But that night I knew I wanted to live.

We remained for a few days while we conducted med checks, gave trainings run by the FBR medics, and distributed donations of clothes and other needed items to civilians. Unlike the Karen, who were Christian, the Shan were Buddhist. I was glad to see that the FBR made good on their promise to help all ethnic minorities regardless of religion. Other than a few prayers between our members, there was no proselytizing of any kind.

We participated in a talk on farming and animal husbandry, helped set up schools for children, and watched soldiers diligently training in the fields. At one point, my tiger-handed friend urged me to join him in jumping jacks.

I kept sleeping in my hammock suspended between the two trucks and never saw any sign of a tiger—but every night I'd hear packs of wild dogs roaming the darkness, howling and running and sometimes fighting.

On the last night, the night before we would head back into the jungle and over the cinematic roads and on and on to Chiang Mai, I lay in my hammock looking up at the stars. I'd gotten so used to hearing the wild dogs that I paid them no attention.

Suddenly a giant *BOOM!* echoed from the jungle, followed by a brief, stark moment of stillness, immediately crowded out by the frenzied yipping and yowling and barking of the injured dogs. The pack had hit a landmine. The next day, as we walked through the jungle, I was more careful than ever where I stepped.

OTHER THINGS HAPPENED during my time in Southeast Asia, like when I finally made my way to Bhutan, which I had originally envisioned being a far easier trip than it was, as if going to Asia was like visiting New York, and I had decided to call up an old friend in Queens while staying in Brooklyn. No one will be surprised to hear that it was not so. Especially if you were in Thailand and this old friend, Jigme Wangchuck, whom you wanted to visit, lived in Bhutan. Oh, and he was, at the time, the crown prince. But eventually

I did go to Bhutan and saw Jigme, who gave me a sword, which is a story for another time.

FBR founder Dave Eubank came back to Thailand right before I left. We all went out to the bar by the storehouse, the one owned by the two sisters. I was happy to finally meet him, after having dinner with his parents at their home outside of Chiang Mai and becoming friends with Laurie, his sister. It was the perfect time, the end of it all: I felt like I'd done the organization right—I'd worked hard and contributed whenever possible. What I had accomplished might have been minor, but it was not superficial.

Dave had a self-contained but strong presence, his energy all the more powerful for being condensed into his wiry, rangy body. He talked a lot of FBR business, but also about his family, how his daughters went horseback riding in country. I started sharing about my trip to Bhutan.

Dave interjected, "You're friends with the crown prince of Bhutan?" His gaze was straightforward and direct, but revealed nothing.

I was straightforward too. "Yes," I said.

"Well, we're not supposed to be a fan of monarchs, Isaac . . . but okay."

What I remember best was Dave's utter clarity of purpose. His belief in what he and FBR did was so firm that others could, and did, lean on it. I desperately wanted that kind of certainty too.

ALL TOO SOON, my visa was about to run out, and it was time to go home. Steve Gumaer and I had one of our last talks. I'm not sure where it was or what we were doing—maybe he was even driving me to the airport—but I still remember the moment.

Steve asked, "Are you going to come back?"

I gave my true heart's answer and spoke in all honesty. "I don't know how I could do anything but," I said. "How could I know about everything that's happening here and just . . . go on about my life?"

Yet that's exactly what I did.

Years later, in 2017, I was living in New York and working at my desk when I came across a viral video of an American aid worker running through ISIS gunfire in Mosul to save a little girl. It was Dave Eubank, who still somehow looked exactly the same—rangy, strong. The FBR is now global, in Iraq and Syria and other regions, while continuing their work in country, where they also provide aid to ethnic minorities like the Rohingya, a Muslim group under attack by the current Burmese government.

While writing this piece, I looked back at the chronicle of emails and journals from this era of my life—the *me* of the past, different enough to be a complete stranger, everything that was wrong with him still shining through with brutal clarity. But worst of all, I am still able to recognize that stranger.

A portrait formed of a willful, impressionable young man who meant well. Who clung to damage because he thought healing was impossible. Who was smart, but thought he was dumb, but underneath that *knew* he was smart, which added up to: shoulders with chips on chips on chips on them. He thought he knew what he was doing, and often didn't see how the people in his life were trying to help him. I read so many emails from friends asking me why I was going to Burma when there was plenty of work that needed doing right here in the U.S., in the Bay Area, where I already lived.

All of that I had expected. But here's one thing I was surprised to find, a little brick that my memory had moved into another spot, just to neaten up the story I was telling myself:

The motorcycle anecdote, the one at the beginning of this piece? It happened *after* I returned from Burma. I wanted to die before I left the States, then in Thailand and Burma I was so brilliantly happy—brimming with both purpose and joy— and then I came back and life happened and my ex and I broke up and I bought a motorcycle and rode seventy miles to San Francisco in a state of utter blackout and I had to figure out again how not to want to die. Which is to say, some days you are happy to be alive, and you know you'll never forget the feeling or lose the knack. And other days you do forget; you *do* lose it. Nothing happens in order, and you have to do it over and over again.

This is all I can say: I know I want to live now, in a way that I didn't want to live back in my twenties, either before or after my time with FBR. I know that I enjoyed helping a group of people who, through their love of God, helped others. And I know that I have questions about what it actually meant for me to be there. One of the old emails I found came from a college friend who was particularly clear and scathing and honest, and—most of all—caring and concerned about me. He wrote, "I get why the medics are there and I get why the journalists are there . . . Why are you there?" I wrote back it was important for FBR to have another set of hands, and it was. But I also know that I was looking for a reason to live, which is not something a white boy needs to fly halfway around the world to find. There was no reason for me to be in a war zone.

Should I have been helping others participate in a civil war I had no right to be in? A dishwasher with no training? No. What about the Christians who believe God has chosen them to help their Karen brethren and other oppressed ethnic minorities? That's not for me to say. On the one hand, I'm not comfortable with people going out to find their war. On the other hand, I know the small girl in Mosul from the video—or many of the thousands upon thousands of people the Eubanks and their followers have helped around the world—was in such need of help that she didn't really care where the help was coming from and was not in a position to reject it.

I think about the parable of the little girl and the starfish told to me by a grandparent, though I can't remember which. A young girl walks along a beach on which thousands of starfish have washed up during a terrible storm. She begins picking up the starfish, one by one, and throwing them back into the sea. An old man walks down to the beach and asks the young girl, "Why are you doing this? Look at how many starfish there are. You cannot possibly begin to make a difference." The girl pays the man no mind and picks up another starfish and throws it back into the waves. Then she says to the old man, "It made a difference to that one."

For many years after, I longed to return to FBR. In fact, when I left, my plan was to get a one-year visa and return to Thailand as quickly as possible, but then as I was saving up money I published my first piece of writing, which turned into my first "real" writing job, which turned into another and then another. One year became three and then ten, and it has not stopped from there.

Because I longed for clarity like Dave Eubanks's so badly, it has been hard sometimes to realize that all the learning and maturing I've done since my twenties has widened and crowded the whole tapestry, adding doubt and confusion. Which is also wisdom, so I could never wish to know less, to give that up just to try and feel more comfortable with myself.

I have to view my time in Burma differently now and understand that no matter how much pain I was in, I had used the real grief and real pain and real war of others as a backdrop for my stumbling search for meaning and purpose. By volunteering in Thailand and Burma, by putting myself in illegal and sometimes dangerous situations, I got to have my white-boy adventure-tourism cake and eat it too.

Yet I would be taking comfort in another kind of too-simple clarity to say that was the whole story, and I should not have volunteered with the FBR in Burma. That my self-ishness had been a pure selfishness that only took and never gave. I still believe I did help, in my small ways: I stuffed envelopes; I packed supplies and sewed the bags; I drove trucks. And perhaps my whiteness helped me to illegally smuggle truckloads of medical and other necessary supplies to groups of people who needed them without delays or hitches, because I was never being stopped or questioned.

Maybe some of the people in the IDP camps were grateful to know there were people out there who saw what was happening to them, and cared, and tried to do what they could; maybe there were some who were angry that these white people could dip in and out and help whenever they wanted in ways that suited them and disappear at other times.

White people who could act with a disregard for the domino-effect consequences because it wouldn't affect them, all the while imposing a specific kind of Christianity on those they wanted to help. Maybe some thought all of these things at once, plus more, or something different altogether. People are not starfish. To truly help involves so much more complexity than the simple motion of picking up a starfish and throwing it into the sea.

But the answer is not to do nothing, at least that's what I've come to believe. You might take longer to consider and investigate and learn than I did, and you might choose differently from me, and ultimately you might still forever feel an overwhelming unease about what you're doing. There are many ways to help, many ways to hurt, and many ways to do both, but there is no way to be perfect. The blinding clarity of the sword and the shield is marvelous and bracing, but I could never truly accept it.

I know that for the rest of my life I will, from time to time, think that the world would be better off without me. But it's happening less as I get older. I will always be trying to stop wondering what exactly I am good for, to instead make peace with the fact that I deserve to be alive and, from that more calm and steady place, will be better able to wrestle with what I can do for myself and others without needing the crutch of certainty.

TOWARD THE END of my stay in Thailand, my ex came to visit. We took my 125cc motor scooter all over the county, from Chiang Mai to Mae Sot to Bangkok and down to

Phuket. Then, under pouring rain, we rode exhausted toward a train station that would return us and the bike up north. We didn't know that fresh roadwork had the new asphalt leaching oil until our bike hit the slick. We crashed and crashed hard, the oil causing us to slide down the road at tremendous speed. Although we were only wearing T-shirts and jeans, we came out with mere scrapes and bruises, as the oil that had caused the accident had also miraculously spared us from the worst of the friction. Trucks rushed past us as we righted the bike. We sat for a long time there on the side of the road, breathing harshly, wide eyed.

Me, happy to be alive.

The Armory

At eleven years old, my friend Brandon and I knew far more about death than sex. Brandon's single mother was a nurse who provided in-home care, which meant that she and Brandon often lived temporarily with her patients. That year, they were staying with the oldest person in town, a skinny, frail woman who never got out of bed as she smoked and drank her days away. Brandon's mother had long since given up on trying to take away her cigarettes or alcohol. The woman was over a hundred years old.

Leaning against the wall of her bedroom was a gold-colored cane. Once, she told me and Brandon that the cane had been given to her when the previous oldest person in town had died.

"It's like a piece of shit trophy that says, 'Congrats. You're next,'" she said, laughing and coughing and laughing again.

Brandon and I laughed with her. We weren't scared or weirded out. After all, we already knew plenty about dying and death. We knew what it looked like; we knew that it was closer than we thought; we knew you just had to joke about it sometimes.

The sum total of what we knew about sex, on the other hand, came from R-rated movies and an old copy of *The Massage Book* by George Downing, which Brandon's mom kept on a high shelf in their house. Though the book was full of illustrations of nude women, the drawings were small and black-and-white and lacked any kind of significant detail. Looking for something sexy in *The Massage Book* was like chewing on Starburst wrappers when you craved steak. But we tried.

Sometime that year two sex educators visited our sixth grade class. They separated the girls and boys into two rooms. The boys' sex educator showed our half of the class how to put a condom on a banana and then left. We didn't have a chance to ask questions, even if we had wanted to do so in front of the other boys, which we absolutely did not.

If anything, this visit had confused us even more. Why were the girls and boys separated? Why were the boys shown our own anatomy (albeit a not incredibly accurate fruit-based version) when that's the anatomy we knew the most about? Why was a condom so important, and why teach us how to use one if we had no idea what it was preventing?

It will come as no surprise that more than a few of my classmates would become parents before they became adults.

Since the sex educators weren't going to help us learn about sex, we realized, we were going to have to do it ourselves.

Brandon thought he had a solution. Next door to the oldest person in town lived an elderly man who looked like he might be next in line for the gold cane. Brandon, prompted by his mother, had recently gone over to the old man's house to help him stack wood for the coming winter in his basement.

That was where Brandon saw it. "It was like a mountain of porn, I'm telling you," he said. "Hundreds, hell, maybe *thousands* of magazines. All there in his basement. Boxes and boxes of the stuff."

We figured the old man wouldn't notice if a few magazines went missing, and came up with a plan. Since his basement window was big enough for us to squeeze through, it would be easy to sneak in and take our pick from the old man's prodigious sixties, seventies, and eighties porn collection.

Which is exactly what we did, after watching and waiting for the old man to go on his daily walk, although his hearing was so bad that we probably could have pulled off the heist even with him inside the house. The whole thing went off without a hitch. We used the wood pile to climb down from the basement window, and then back up again after we'd made our hurried selections and folded the magazines under our shirts.

The rest of the afternoon we spent in Brandon's temporary bedroom in the old woman's house, gazing upon pages and pages of mesmerizing naked women, familiarizing ourselves with their bodies and their stated likes and dislikes, as if we could discover the secret to being loved. Among the magazines were *Playboy*s and *Hustler*s, as well as more obscure publications whose names now escape me. I remember that Brandon and I were surprised to find cartoons in some of the magazines, not to mention unexpectedly long and wordy articles and interviews. We traded issues and took turns going into the bathroom, protective of our ill-gotten treasure and alert for any creaks that could be Brandon's mother or one of his siblings walking up the wooden stairs.

In hindsight it was a bit of a magical day. One that we would repeat many times after, stealing more issues from the old man in the coming months as we got bored with the magazines we had, eventually selling ones we grew tired of to other kids in our class.

But that business plan wouldn't last long. Brandon and I, both born in 1983, didn't know it yet, but we belonged to a very special age group—those who had begun their adolescence knowing analog porn, only to have everything change with the arrival of the internet.

WHEN THE INTERNET took over, I was fourteen and living with twenty-nine other fourteen-year-old boys in my dormitory at a small New England boarding school. Every student at the school was assigned an email account upon arriving to campus; a 3D animation of a dancing baby had become the world's first viral meme despite nobody yet knowing the terms "viral" or "meme"; and internet pornography was already, unsurprisingly, everywhere. Especially in our dorm rooms, where all thirty of us had our own internet-connected computer.

There's an issue of *Time* magazine from 1995 with an unsettling cover: A young boy is sitting at a keyboard, his face bathed in the bright, chilly light of the screen, eyes opened wide in a mix of horror and fascination. Below his face is a headline in big, fearmongering letters: CYBERPORN.

By 1996 President Clinton had signed the Communications Decency Act into law, spurred by anti-porn activists and reactionary "family values" groups. Obviously the boys in my dormitory were not the only people watching porn online. Given any kind of new technological advancement, be it the printing press, longer-lasting pigments, or the camcorder, it is only a matter of time before humankind uses it to make and distribute porn. Why should the internet be any different? In fact, many of the functions of the internet we enjoy today—images, videos, GIFs, even the exchange of money—were pioneered by porn sites.

At the time, my classmates and I didn't know about any of that. All we knew was that one kid down the hall knew about a website called Dr. Bizzaro that had every pornographic photo you could ever wish to see, for free. All we knew was that we were glad that the internet had come along just in time to (temporarily) relieve us of our unbearable horniness.

When we'd first arrived on campus freshman year, we had been shy and timid—not just because we were meeting new classmates, but also because we had to live with each other. We had to adjust to being in a group setting, pretty much all the time. Walking to the showers (which thankfully had individual stalls), we kept our towels wrapped tightly around our bodies, though as we stood in line and waited for our turn, it was hard not to notice who among us was developing more quickly than the others.

But some boys, like Sam Jones, took great pains to keep their bodies hidden. Sam was chubby, with long, stringy blonde hair. All I knew about Sam was that he was nerdy, liked computers, and kept to himself. Though we'd been at school for only a couple of weeks, a pecking order was already forming, and Sam was nowhere near the top of it, or even the middle.

Something that didn't help his social standing was the way he wore both a robe *and* pajamas while waiting in line for the shower, conspicuous among all of us with towels around our waists. Once Dan Doyle, a hockey player who was sixteen yet somehow still a freshman like the rest of us (some mysterious reason having to do with grades and eligibility), jeered at Sam. "What, afraid we'll all see your dick?"

Sam didn't respond. A shower opened up and he stepped inside, still in his robe and pajamas, and drew the curtain shut. The whole moment was as pure a dumb, shitty bullying scene out of some eighties teen film as you could get. Which made what followed that much sweeter.

It was a couple of months into the school year, and the boys in my dorm had grown less shy. Some of us walked to the showers naked. This one guy gave everyone a demonstration of "dick puppetry," long before the hit show in Vegas, saying, "This one's the bulldog. This is the brain," and so on. It was exactly how you'd picture it.

By then, everyone had pretty much come to terms with the fact that privacy was impossible. We all watched porn together, and at least a few roommates would jerk off in the same room. My roommate Jon and I didn't watch videos together—the two of us were analog boys in a bright digital future—but sometimes while lying in our bunks we'd take turns telling stories while the other masturbated. Just like the *Decameron*.

A bunch of us were hanging out one day when Jon burst in and said, "Uh, you guys should come see this." He wouldn't tell us what, just that we needed to see whatever was in Sam Jones's room. But as we walked down the long, cold dormitory hallway, I thought I knew what to expect. I was wrong.

Sam was in his room, looking quite a bit like a deer in headlights. Porn was still up on the computer screen, but oddly enough it was no longer the center of attention.

"Show them what you showed me," Jon said to him.

Sam hesitated. "Are you sure?"

"C'mon, you should be *proud*."

So Sam unzipped his pants and took his dick out. Simply, his dick was the largest dick that any of us had ever seen, in real life *or* porn.

Sam could sense that we were impressed. "Wanna see something?" he said.

We thought we already had, but, damn, okay, sure.

That's when Sam Jones sucked his own dick in front of us. The most shocking part—other than the fact that this was literally happening—was how easy it was for him. Despite having a belly big enough to get in the way, Sam didn't need to roll around on the floor, or wrench his legs over his head, or contort in any kind of fancy, uncomfortable position to achieve this feat. No—he merely bent his head, placed his dick in his mouth, and went for it.

What I didn't know at that time—a time during which I immersed myself in porn at boarding school, watched it with the other students there (though porn-watching as a group activity would fizzle out early into sophomore year, as societal homophobia so urgently pressed upon young men in the nineties began to take hold), and would later watch it at college as streaming videos became more accessible—what I couldn't possibly have suspected was that by the time I was in my midtwenties, I would find myself on the other side. Not as a viewer, not as a watcher, but as a doer, a participant, a performer.

THE FIRST TIME I walked past the Armory in San Francisco, it was night. The streetlights that lined Mission Street were all busted, and I felt small and alone next to the giant graffiti-covered building, which was surrounded by broken bottles and loomed ominously against the black sky.

It was 2006 and I was twenty-three. I'd moved from the East Coast a few months earlier. A couple of blocks from the overpass on Fourteenth Street and Mission wasn't the best place for a newcomer to be in those days, but I was such a newcomer that I didn't know that yet.

The Armory was colossal, taking up an entire city block, and a long one, at that. Made of brick, and boasting parapets, turrets, and an enormous arched roof over what had once served as parade grounds, the building had been built between 1912 and 1914 and originally housed an arsenal for the United States National Guard. In the 1940s, it had been converted to a sports venue, where the drill court would be filled with chairs and bleachers so locals could come watch prize-fight boxing matches.

By the time I strolled past the Armory in 2006, it had been empty for thirty years, despite the fact that it had been registered as a historical landmark in 1978. It hadn't gone completely unused, however: Several spaceship-interior scenes for *Star Wars: The Empire Strikes Back* had been filmed there. And occasionally the inner court, useful for its vastness, had been used for set construction and rehearsals by the San Francisco Opera, but even that came to an end by the mid-1990s.

Now the Armory was all but abandoned, save for the numerous squatters who made the large structure their home. Skateboarders did tricks on the steps of the main entrance, a spot that became one of San Francisco's most famous skate locations. It was known as "3 Up, 3 Down" because of the number of stairs.

I would learn the building's history later, when I was making porn there and when I assisted with the shoot of a nonporn feature film starring some recognizable Hollywood names, all in the same space where the Millennium Falcon scenes had been filmed (which never failed to delight my *Star Wars*–loving soul).

Before all of that happened, though, all I knew was that the Armory was right near the dilapidated apartment building where I'd just gotten a room. This particular block, presided over by an abandoned castle among broken streetlights, made me a little nervous at first.

But soon things began to change. By the following year, the streetlights were working again. Trees were planted along the sidewalk. And then the broken bottles and graffiti vanished and the front steps were cleaned up (luckily the skateboarders got to stay).

Apparently, after a heated community debate, a porn company called Kink.com had bought the Armory. The owner of Kink.com was Peter Acworth, a man I would meet very soon.

THE THING ABOUT San Francisco is that it's a beautiful city filled with beautiful people that has a long history of attracting roughnecks, adventurers, and weirdos. "The mad ones," as Kerouac said in *On the Road.*

Not yet fully bulldozed by tech money, the San Francisco I fell in love with shortly after moving there shared a lot of similarities with Kerouac's San Francisco. Sure, there had been changes too; that's what half a century will do. But you still got the bay boats, the late nights, the food and nightlife clustered with the hills of Chinatown and North Beach. The docks down by the water and, merely a bridge away, all the wilderness you could ever want.

Another thing that hadn't changed was that San Francisco was small: Seven miles by seven miles. With only so many places to go, groups tended to overlap—you got your anarchist vegan hackers on my grandmas operating a tamale cart! You got your hair metal enthusiasts on my yogi Eastern philosophers! And you got your skateboarding and BMX boys all over everything.

I loved that aspect of that city. By 2009, between hanging out at Zeitgeist and slowly making inroads with the local literary community, I'd started making friends with numerous sex workers who were also writers, and writers who were also drinkers, and drinkers who were also sex workers, and more than a few who were all three.

Lorelei Lee was an up-and-coming writer and an award-winning porn star. There were fan websites and stalkers and everything that came with being the center of strangers' fantasies, but I didn't know any of that yet. I saw them read at a place called the Make-Out Room. Onstage, dressed in pink, their ice-blonde hair swooped over their shoulder. Soon after that we became friends, and they brought me along to a fancy dinner at a sushi restaurant with a big group of people from the San Francisco sex worker community.

I fell into conversation with a man sitting across the table from me, who introduced himself as Tomcat. Tomcat was the first out trans man I'd ever knowingly had a conversation with, and he worked as a porn director at Kink. He was handsome in a simple uniform of a white T-shirt and jeans and tattoos. We talked about his work, and I peppered him with questions while ordering more sake and beer.

A slight man with bright blue eyes and a British accent stood up at the end of the table and asked the waiter to bring more food. "Who is that?" I asked Tomcat.

"That's Peter. You don't know who Peter is?"

". . . No?"

"Well, firstly, he's the one paying for your meal. Also, Peter is my boss."

"He runs Kink?"

"Yep," Tomcat said, flashing me a quick smile. "Peter loves to party, loves kinky sex, and he learned how to make money off the things he loves."

Tomcat explained that when Peter was a PhD candidate at a prestigious university, he decided to get involved with the porn industry. Rumor was that he had read a story about a firefighter back in the U.K. who made a ton of money after starting his own porn site.

So Peter started Hogtied.com. Instead of producing the porn himself, he licensed porn from other bondage-focused producers. When Hogtied.com became a hit, he abandoned his graduate studies to focus on the site. Not long after, he moved to San Francisco and began producing his own content, sometimes participating in the videos himself.

By the early 2000s Peter owned an array of sites—including the popular Fucking Machines, which Tomcat operated—and had created an umbrella group for all of his digital production companies: Kink.com. In late 2006, Acworth announced that he was purchasing the San Francisco Armory.

"If you ever want to come visit," Tomcat said, "I'd love to give you a tour."

TOMCAT WAS AS good as his word. I met him at the front desk of the Armory, where I was given a guest pass. The inside of the building had been completely cleaned up and renovated. Though it still had an old-fashioned grandeur, it looked sparkling new, from the newly polished mosaic floors to the restored woodwork and moldings.

"This is where we edit the videos," Tomcat said, walking me through a large open-floor-plan office that looked like any other tech startup, with workstations on metal desks, stacked right next to each other. Employees walked by wearing black Kink.com shirts emblazoned with the logo, a red K with a devil's tail attached.

I could have easily been in an office at Facebook, Twitter, or LinkedIn, except the other floors were filled with film sets. Bedrooms. Classrooms. Dungeons. In the basement were cages and chains, plus a full bar that was technically operational and sometimes was. There were also plenty of cameras and hand sanitizer and robes and towels. I saw shower rooms from back when the Armory still housed military personnel that were also sets, and ones that were just plain shower rooms.

Tomcat also took me below the lower levels, into a dark room where I heard running water and, as my eyes adjusted to the dark, saw a river.

"What's *that*?"

"That, my friend, is Mission Creek, the water source for the Mission Dolores religious settlement way back in the day. Over the years it's been built over, all throughout the Mission and San Francisco. This is the only place you can see it. The soldiers kept access to it in case the Amory was ever held under siege."

We left and reemerged in a long hallway. Each of the rooms had a red light bulb outside its door. Tomcat pointed to one that was glowing. "If the red light bulb is on, don't go in."

He showed me a large green and white arena with a huge wrestling ring in the center of the room. "This is where we shoot Ultimate Surrender," Tomcat said. He explained that Ultimate Surrender was erotic wrestling, where the winner fucks the loser. Ultimate Surrender was just one of the twenty-six channels under the Kink.com umbrella, along with Fucking Machines, Bound Gods, TS Seduction, Naked Kombat, Public Disgrace, Hardcore Gangbangs, and many others.

"You know," Tomcat said, "you can sign up to be an audience member for the Ultimate Surrender shows, if you want."

"Do you get paid?"

Tomcat laughed. "Uh, *no*. In fact, we should probably be charging money for tickets, but that's another conversation. But . . . if you are interested in getting paid to do model work, I know who you could talk to."

He walked me around the building until we found Princess Donna. She had been at the sushi dinner, but we hadn't talked much.

Tomcat said, "Princess, you think this guy could make a decent extra?"

Princess Donna wasn't tall but she had a *tallness* to her. Sure, her shoes helped, but it was mainly her attitude—the sharp elegance and regal bearing that made me immediately understand why everyone called her "Princess."

She looked me up and down. "Just had someone cancel. Could he do the van shoot?"

THE DAY OF the van shoot was sunny, even down by the water—one of those fogless days when San Francisco's California splendor is on full display. I'd been driving around the Dogpatch on my motorcycle for over half an hour, unfamiliar with the neighborhood of abandoned docks and empty industrial buildings. When I finally arrived at the shoot, on a street that was empty save for a few lonely bags of uncollected trash and the aforementioned van, a woman walked toward me and didn't even wait until I'd gotten my helmet off to tell me that I was late.

"Come on," she continued. "Donna and Ray are already in the van. Are you tested?"

"Tested?"

"STD test. With a clinic we trust. In the past week. You should have paperwork."

"Uh, I got an STD test a few months ago," I offered, already feeling lost.

"Yeah. No. That doesn't cut it. Here's the deal: You can watch. You can touch. You can talk. But nothing else, okay? Only hand stuff."

I stammered my agreement as my mind churned, trying to figure out what "hand stuff" entailed.

The woman stopped. For the first time, she looked me full in the face, obviously checking if I was, indeed, *okay.*

"Good," she said after a brief moment, and opened the van door.

Inside was Princess Donna, in full makeup and her usual work uniform of skin-tight, jet-black, low-cut latex. Crammed in next to her was a man with a high-and-tight buzz cut whose body was a mountain of muscle. His height required him to slouch, even though he was already sitting on the floor of the van, where all of the back seats had been removed.

Donna gave me a slight nod of recognition and an even slighter smile. "Let's get to it," she said. Not only was Donna the star, but she was also the director.

The cameraman scrambled gracefully over the front passenger seat and into the back with us, gently pushing me into frame as he did so. The muscular man started unbuttoning his shirt and growled at Donna, "You ready to get fucked, bitch?"

And so it began.

There was no plot to speak of, but the scene was plenty interesting enough without it, focusing on two extremely attractive people going at it in the back of a van, as a fully clothed young man in his twenties who was trying not to look too wide-eyed (and was therefore even more obviously so) looked on, occasionally reaching out to softly stroke the woman's breasts and back and body. At one point, the man told me, "Choke her. Choke her!" So I tentatively put my hands around Donna's neck and squeezed as gently as possible, scared that I might hurt her, as if she didn't clearly have all the power in the room—er, van. The two actors were far too professional to roll their eyes and interrupt the scene, but did their best to act around my poor performance.

I didn't know it at the time, but Kink hired more women and femme directors than most other major porn companies and required performers to wear condoms during any penetrative sex scenes—making it one of the more progressive studios in the industry.

Whenever Donna yelled, "Cut!" that was *it*. Immediately the camera would be turned off and pointed downward and immediately the man would stop whatever he was doing to move off and away from her, lifting his hands and putting them on his head (so I did the same). Immediately his whole demeanor would transform, from menacing and demanding to calm and receptive. All this, it seemed, before the word had even fully left her mouth.

My mind flashed back to all the sex education I'd barely received as a child. Where had there been any discussion of consent—whatsoever? Instead, we had been taught the phrase "No means no" alongside society's toxic messaging that "No" didn't always count depending on who said it or when or why or how, as evidenced by all the rom-coms that rewarded the male lead's persistence, and his ability to kiss without asking and show up without being invited.

Here in the van, Donna's "No"—in this case, "Cut!"—meant no in the most certain terms. It meant no, and it meant "You will cease doing whatever you were doing right now and place your hands where I can see them and move away from me and await further instructions."

"You need something, Donna? A towel? Some water?" The first time I heard the man speak out of character, his voice was completely transformed. From gritty and gravelly, like a pile of rocks in a cement mixer, to soft and diffident—and about five octaves higher.

He noticed me noticing. "What? You never heard of gay for pay?" the giant asked while gently pushing me farther away from Donna so she could have more space. "Well, it goes both ways, baby."

After the filming finished, Donna and I stepped out of the van and back into the empty street. The sun was still bright, but lower in the sky than before.

The woman who had greeted me earlier handed me a clipboard with a form that I almost certainly should have been asked to sign before filming. I signed the waiver with the attention to detail most twentysomethings have when it comes to bureaucracy.

Donna looked both completely out of place and right at home standing in the middle of the street in her robe, her latex outfit still on floor of the van. She had slipped back into her high heels. "Not bad," she said. "Although you can choke harder next time."

The straight-for-pay muscle man, whose name was Ray, emerged from the van and stretched.

"You want to get paid more next time?" Donna asked me.

"Yeah!" I said, with the eagerness of a golden retriever.

"Get tested beforehand. I'll email you what you need to know, and then I'll reach out about an upcoming shoot. Pay is three hundred dollars a pop."

"What's a 'pop'?" I asked without thinking.

Donna and Ray's laughter echoed out over the empty docks and into the Bay.

AFTER THAT, I was in. I filled out more paperwork, including a checklist of sexual acts I was comfortable performing on camera, and picked a stage name. I never stuck to one—like Frank Abagnale Jr. in the book *Catch Me If You Can*—Okay, the names I used were all aliases from *Catch Me If You Can*. Anyway, I made videos and got paid. Three hundred dollars a pop. Which—in case it took you as long as me to figure out—was every time I came on camera.

Was I good at it? Not particularly. As my new friend Ray put it, "It takes a lot to make it in this industry, and *you*," he said, giving me a once-over, "you're gonna have to put in a lot of effort." So I did, with help along the way from the likes of Tomcat, Lorelei, and Princess Donna.

The money added up pretty fast, going toward rent and paying for a new computer, since all of my usual gigs combined weren't fully cutting it—but it would be a lie to say I was in it for the money. Sure, I was broke. But that's not why I chose to do porn.

The fact is, I enjoyed porn. Was a consumer of porn. Had bonding relationships in my early teens that were based on the consumption of porn and communal jerking off, starting with magazines, and then—with the introduction of the internet—JPEGs and streaming videos. Technically, my work at Kink wasn't even my first time making money in this industry: I'd broken into an old man's basement and scaled a pile of wood to steal his magazines, which I would later sell. I'd consumed a whole boatload of porn, and now the opportunity to participate in its creation had presented itself. Who was I to say no? Or put another way, why would I?

I've always been on Team Mary Magdalene.

The fact of the matter is, like in any community, it came down to the people. Although Ray turned out to live in L.A. so we didn't encounter each other often, Princess Donna, Lorelei, and Tomcat became a constant in my life at a time when nothing else was. My relationships kept falling apart, surely not helped by the amount of time I was spending in San Francisco bars. My days working at Zeitgeist were over by then, but my days spent drinking all day there—or anywhere else in the city—were not.

Kink was a different scene, a new part of the city revealing itself to me. I had never felt comfortable in my own skin; here were people who very much did. I had never really been comfortable talking about sex—a mix of miseducation and Catholic guilt. Here were people who managed to make a living from it.

Tomcat, who is from Canada, would invite me over to his house for a big Canadian Thanksgiving feast every October, where guests were required to give brief pro-Canadian presentations. He accompanied me on weekend benders from time to time, but was always sure to get us both home safe. He cut my hair occasionally and took one of my favorite photographs of me: My eyes are blurry and I'm washed out by light pouring through a barroom window, but the way Tomcat frames the shot, a bottle of beer in front of me, there's a certain kind of hope to it. That photo made me feel like he saw me in a way that no one else had.

Lorelei and I dated for a short time, although the word "dated" is probably too serious and one-sided (my side). We were friends before and during, and so we seamlessly remained friends after, bonding over our difficult childhoods and our love of books and writing and simply just enjoying being around each other, whether we were laughing about dogs or having intense debates that I would always lose.

Princess Donna and I worked together the most, me performing and Donna directing. But we became friends, too, and hung out after shoots, like the time I invited her and Lorelei to my horrible dump of an apartment to drink tequila. They looked completely out of place there—like movie stars in some grimy postapocalypse—which embarrassed me, until later when I saw their not-all-that-much-nicer apartments. Even then, however, there was a sensible reason for that. "I'm saving to buy property, Isaac," Donna said. "I've got to think about the future."

Once Donna and I got tattoos together, and while we were getting our work done, she talked the owner of the tattoo shop into letting her film there in the future. Another time she asked me about one of my tattoos, which had been done with a homemade tattoo gun, and figured out how to make her own version using a needle attached to a Hitachi Magic Wand. It worked astonishingly well.

And of course there were the shoots. I participated in shower scenes and classroom scenes, and the mystery around how porn gets made quickly fell away. The schedules, the snacks on set. The lighting changes, the small talk between takes, the off-brand Viagra available to those of us who might need it. "Isaac, hold there for a moment, we need a different angle."

But even as the work became routine, as all work does, the Armory still felt like a special place. Group parties often occurred on the top floor with everyone in masks among elegant, overstuffed chaise longues and ottomans, doms showing off their whip skills and rope knots. It was fantasy made real and then put onto film and turned back into fantasy.

My understanding of sex grew. My horizons—to use that old cliche—expanded. I started to examine sex as an act, taking in the differences between performing sex and being intimate with someone. The more I saw, the more I understood. The more I participated, the more comfortable I became. Here I was, someone who had sex often but rarely talked about it—save those confessions of my youth—slowly learning how to articulate what I was comfortable with, and how to listen to others when they did the same.

I began to feel more confident on camera. Again, not so much in my performance—I was never going to be Ray—but I do remember my shirt eventually coming off a little quicker and my robe dropping a little faster. This was reflected in my personal life too. When the cameras weren't rolling, I found myself less confused by my own body. How it looked. How it felt to hold someone or be held by them. I learned to have the same conversations I'd have before a shoot, but with intimate partners instead of coworkers. I wasn't carrying around a checklist of acts, but I grew more comfortable looking someone in the eye and asking, "So, what are you into?"

KINK.COM GREW OVER the years. Peter Acworth had wanted to create a BDSM Disneyland at the Armory—a Playboy Mansion but with more leather and handcuffs—and for a short time, he did. The company bought a dive bar across the street that was going out of business and turned it into a BDSM-themed cocktail lounge that they used for afterparties and shoots from time to time. More and more businesses, mostly bars and tattoo shops but occasionally even bookstores, agreed to allow Princess Donna and her crew to shoot on location. As Peter had promised when he first bought the Armory, Kink became part of the neighborhood. By the time I left the city, it seemed as though Kink might become a fixture of the Mission District forever.

Years after leaving San Francisco, when I was living in New York, I heard that Peter had gotten in trouble for the alleged shooting of firearms in the historic firing range in the basement of the Armory. When the police made a show of arresting Peter instead of calling him in, they found one gram of cocaine on his person. All charges were later dropped but not before the press ran with it. But that was simply one of many difficulties Kink began to face—and a minor one at that. The larger problems? The Mission was changing. Tech was changing. The things that once worked in the startup porn company's favor began to work against it. The internet was no longer a free and wild place. There were more rules.

More money. Corporations like Google and Facebook began to wield more and more power, and their employees—often young people with large bank accounts—began moving to San Francisco and changing the fabric of the city. Early in 2017, Kink announced it would stop using the Armory for film production. In 2018, ten years after the Armory hosted its first Mission Bazaar, an all-ages art fair featuring local craftspeople, artists, and performers, the Armory was sold to a Chicago-based investment company for $65 million (not bad, given the building was bought in 2006 for $14.5 million). The company plans to turn the building into office space.

I MODELED AT Kink for all of six months. Many people who work in porn only do so for a short time. All told, I participated in maybe a dozen shoots. There was no big realization it was time for me to leave, no exact moment when I decided to stop making porn. Like any other job I held in my twenties, I did it for a while and then moved on to something new. Have I ever watched the videos I was in? Not on purpose, although every once in a blue moon a friend will text me, "Is this . . . you?"

But the videos I was in—they were just the product. What I still hold and treasure to this day is how much I admire the people I worked with and became friends with. Lorelei Lee would become seriously involved with the sex workers' rights movement and continue to publish incredible essays, and eventually get their MFA in creative writing and a law degree from an Ivy League school. Tomcat and Lorelei got married and I attended their marvelous ceremony, which was held at a quintessentially Californian venue that still had bullets in the door from a cowboy-era shootout. Now many of us live in New York, and we still gather for Canadian Thanksgiving.

The idea of a "chosen family" is a queer concept, so it makes sense that I—a cis straight man—learned about it first-hand in this very queer space in San Francisco. I might not have felt at home with my biological family, whom I wasn't in contact with at the time, but I was not lost. I could find people who would care for me, and whom I could care for.

It's strange—when you grow up in a house with your parents, when you go to church regularly, you're supposed to feel safe in these spaces. To *be* safe. Except I hadn't, and I wasn't. I did find safety, and love, and friendship, and fun in a massive brick BDSM porn compound, the same way I did in bars and bookstores and in wandering the streets of the Bay Area. "The mad ones," as it turns out, are the people who will love you and care for you without judgment so long as you are deserving of it and you give the same back.

I STILL WATCH lots of porn. Not as much as I did when I was fourteen, but it's still a part of my life, which I think is true for many, many people. You can hide sex away or laugh at it or be afraid of it or pretend it doesn't exist, but it doesn't change that humans will always be interested in it, no matter what the hypocrites say. As someone who barely received any sex education as an adolescent, I think that's a good thing.

When I watch porn, there's the actual sex part, obviously, but there's also an awareness of what's not onscreen. What

I remember best from my time doing porn are all the moments between takes, before and after the shoots. The laughter, eating pizza while wearing robes in the dark basement rooms of the Armory. The barbecues and going to the pride parade together. Dykes on Bikes. I owe so much to sex workers when it comes to being more open about sex. About knowing how to talk about sex. And my understanding of consent—not just the idea of consent, but the practice. How to respond correctly to a no or "Cut!" or a safe word, which is to say: Never, ever less than fully and immediately. How to discuss the sex you're about to have, even if you feel embarrassed or awkward talking about it. How to identify all the ways in which people coerce or pressure or push—sometimes without consciously knowing it—and not do those things. And how to have a conversation with a partner about what I want, and ask them the same.

If society protected, respected, listened to, and learned from sex workers—well, then, sex education might actually stand a chance of being useful. And we all might be a little better at having those important conversations. Those difficult conversations, possibly even the ones that aren't about sex. Because in the end, what I'm talking about is communication. Feeling safe. Knowing how to state, clearly, what you are feeling, and maybe even why.

Imagine if violent homes came with safe words.

Everybody stop.

Hands on your head.

Quiet on the set, please.

High for the Holidays

"Polé, polé. Slowly, slowly."

For hours now, my sister, my father, and I have been climbing in the darkness. Rock and glacial snow crunch under our boots. Ahead of us our guide Habibu shuffles his feet. He stops every twenty yards to turn and shine a flashlight onto my sister. Her face is blue.

It's before dawn on Christmas morning and we're on day seven of our climb up Mount Kilimanjaro. We had left camp at ten P.M. the night before, planning to summit at sunrise. At first this had seemed entirely possible. My father, old but strong, had showed no signs of fatigue. Neither had I, despite a number of bad habits that were cautioned against in the guidebook: *Do you exercise?* No. *Do you smoke?* Yes. *Do you drink?* With extreme prejudice.

My sister is a marathon runner and a vegetarian. Yet it was

she who started falling back into me every time we came to a large rock, as if she were on a weekend bender.

"Maybe we should turn around?" I say.

Our guide stops again and shines his light into my sister's eyes. "Stick out your tongue." She sticks it out, as she had at me so many times when we were younger.

"No," he finally says. "We can keep going. Polé, polé. Slowly, slowly." So we continue our stumble up the mountain.

CHRISTMAS ON KILIMANJARO is the first holiday I've spent with family in seven years. My sister's email was short and to the point: "I want to climb Mount Kilimanjaro. You should come. I'll pay." Whenever it came time to visit family, crying poverty was my favorite excuse. But this wasn't your regular Christmas at home—this would be Christmas on a mountain. With my sister. My half-sister, actually, whom I hadn't seen much of since we were little, visiting each other occasionally while growing up in separate homes on separate sides of the state. She was making an effort, and I was getting to the age where I could appreciate that.

"Sure," I wrote back, making a mental note to cut back on my smoking. "Just you and me."

Our family tree isn't so much a tree as a thicket. My sister is my father's daughter, but not my mother's. My brother is my mother's son, but not my father's. Their union—and my birth—had robbed my half-sister of her father and my half-brother of his mother. It had also given me two half-siblings whom I loved wholly.

Just weeks before we were supposed to fly out from NYC, my sister called. "Dad would like to come, too."

"If you want, I could tell him this is our trip," I said. "That it's about us bonding. I'm not afraid to ask him not to come."

"Why would I want that?" she said.

"Oh. Right." Turned out I was the one who was afraid to have our dad come along.

Suddenly I was eight years old again, trying to block out the noise.

"WE CAN SWITCH places, if you like." My father keeps offering to walk behind her, to catch my sister if she falls backward, and I keep saying I'm fine. She is suffering from altitude sickness. Blurred vision. Dizziness. A headache. She is dehydrated, no matter how much water she drinks.

I can feel that my father is worried. He always worries about us when we are sick. I am worried too. But underneath that worry we both want the same thing: to get up the mountain. Underneath her sickness my sister is no different; she just wants to get to the top.

ONCE MY DAD got into the holiday-plan mix, my mom started getting feisty. "Well, you're already coming east to fly out with your sister and your father," she said. "I just don't understand why you can't come a little earlier for Thanksgiving."

"Ma, I told you. A college friend is getting married in Baltimore that weekend. It's an Indian wedding. Lasts three days."

Thank god for holiday weddings. Any family but your own. I didn't have to think about Kilimanjaro, and I tried not to. After three days of celebrating—dancing the Dandiya Raas and doing my damnedest not to seem too drunk despite leaving the hours-long ceremony to sneak shots with hotel workers—a good friend of mine who had spent his entire college career in the closet and was making up for lost time turned to me and said, "Want to go to a club?"

His date, whom I barely knew, chimed in. "We found a local place advertised on Grindr. 'Down Low After-Hours Gay Hip-Hop.' Downtown Baltimore." And then, inevitably: "Here, take these!"

The first pills took hold before we got there; otherwise we might have just turned around and left. The club was unpromising and sparse. A few men circled each other on the dance floor. Most huddled close to the bar, which sold giant cups of vodka for seven dollars a pour.

"Happy holidays," the bartender said to me as I ordered my third. Eventually the room grew crowded, and soon the pills that we promised ourselves we would slowly take over the course of the night were gone. We bounced together on the dance floor, attracting a crowd so thick I couldn't tell if it was my friend playfully smacking my ass or a stranger with other intentions. Either way, I didn't care.

Since moving to San Francisco, I'd spent every Thanksgiving and Christmas in bars, having heart-to-hearts with strangers who would eventually become friends, friends who would eventually become family. This is how I was most comfortable—drunk and far from home on the holidays. Always happy to talk with people I didn't know.

"Be careful who sees you leaving here." The bouncer opened the door as my friend, his wedding date, and their two new friends spilled into the street. The cab had already been hailed.

"Come with us!" they chorused, but I waved goodbye as they got into the purple-and-white car.

"Hey! You shouldn't walk," the bouncer shouted after me, but I was already off, striding down the street in the direction of my hotel. I've always been good at walking, finding my way around. Putting one foot in front of the other.

"POLÉ, POLÉ. SLOWLY, slowly."

The sun breaks on the glaciers as we walk toward Uhuru Peak, the highest point on Mount Kilimanjaro. My sister is being held up by the guide, but she seems to be improving. Still, we rest every few yards. Japanese tourists walk past us briskly, their hiking poles chipping away at the ice.

Behind me is Foza, a guide who has been with us since he picked us up from the airport. Foza is skinny the way runway models want to be, his biceps the same size as his forearms.

"See," says Foza, "I told you we'd make it." He points at my father. "Babu is strong, and your sister, she is all right."

I look ahead as tourists crowd around the green sign erected by the government of Tanzania, written only in English: CONGRATULATIONS! YOU ARE NOW AT UHURU PEAK, TANZANIA, 5,895 M. A.M.S.L. AFRICA'S HIGHEST POINT. WORLD'S HIGHEST FREE STANDING MOUNTAIN.

We are standing on top of an entire continent. A menagerie of cameras capture smiling faces and a sky that goes on forever. Someone offers my sister tea from a thermos.

"What do we do now?" I ask Foza.

He grins, probably because he's been asked the question so many times before. "Now we go back down."

It took us seven days to climb to the summit of Mount Kilimanjaro. It will take us only two to return to its base.

"MAYBE WE'LL GET together again next year," my sister says before we part ways, back in NYC. "The whole family."

My father and I had shared a tent on our way up Kilimanjaro. He'd farted and pissed in bottles and we'd read books and sat in silence. There had been no great conversation. I hadn't forgiven him, and he didn't ask to be forgiven. We just walked up a mountain together. One foot in front of the other. Either me looking at his back or him looking at mine. He was a different man and I was a different boy. Polé, polé. Slowly, slowly.

Not next year, I think. But maybe soon.

I hug my sister goodbye and immediately go to a tattoo parlor. After that, I spend the next ten hours before my flight at a bar in Red Hook, Brooklyn. After the bar closes for the night, I get to the airport four hours early, but still almost miss my plane out of New York. Being at the airport on time doesn't guarantee that you'll actually make it onto your flight—if you pass out in front of the gate.

"Are you Isaac Fitzgerald?" says the airline employee who, after calling my name multiple times over the intercom, is kind enough to come over and kick me awake. "Hurry up. Doors are closing. Hurry, hurry!"

The year before, my brother and his wife had announced that she was pregnant. I was on the West Coast and wasn't there in person to share their joy. Nor was I there to share their pain when they lost the baby. The three thousand miles between coasts had somehow gone from a distance that allowed me to grow into my own person, away from the shadow of our family history, to a distance that kept me from being part of the new, different family we were becoming. We had all changed. Life had gone on long enough for us to try getting things right. I didn't need to be the guy who drank tequila in the mornings and never saw his parents. For the first time in years, my heart felt pulled toward the Atlantic instead of the Pacific. My sister knew it before I did.

Not long after my father, my sister, and I climbed Kilimanjaro, my brother texted me one word. "Heartbeat." Three months after that I moved back to the East Coast.

That year's Christmas was the first I spent with my family—my full family—in almost a decade. Seven days up. Two days down.

DAYS BEFORE WE climb the mountain, I am in a truck with my father and my sister in the middle of the Serengeti, staring up into a tree. "Be patient," Foza says. "It has its dinner. The leopards take their kill into the tree. Their spots help them hide. How do you say? Camouflage." Foza speaks ten languages. Sometimes he mixes them up. He is a father himself. "Sons are hard," he'd said one day, almost at random.

"Look in the tree," says Foza. "Can you see the leopard?" The Tanzanian sunlight is shining through the large, sparse leaves. Nothing moves. Our necks arch, and our eyes search. "Just be patient," Foza says. "You'll see it."

"Look," Foza says. We stare at the tree, knowing there is a leopard but seeing nothing.

There is a rustle. And then the bones fall from the branches.

When Your Barber Assumes You're a Racist, Too

The second time I saw Gavin McInnes's dick it wasn't my fault. It happened when I was getting a haircut, and the hungoverly chatty barber was telling me about his partly professional and occasionally social relationship with McInnes. If you're lucky enough not to know, McInnes is a founder of *Vice* magazine and Vice Media whose post-Vice career has involved a lot of hate speechifying, denying that said hate speechifying was meant sincerely, and creating a group called the Proud Boys. Give you two guesses what they're proud of.

Now, Nazis who try to keep the fact that they are Nazis kind of secret (despite it being 100 percent obvious) like to use two words. There's "pride," which is invoked whenever they are accused of hate. No, they are just proud! Of being white! That's the only feeling they have about their whiteness!

This charade never lasts for any length of time whatsoever. But, to be fair, "white pride" is shorter than "everybody else hate."

They also love to talk about "humor," as in "the left has no sense of," as if they can brute-force compel people to laugh at jokes that aren't funny, and shame them if they don't. Uhhh-hhhhh, sorry that you're only funny when you fail clown-ishly, which is often? Because you know what is fucking funny? Naming their—in their words—"pro-Western fraternal organization for men who refuse to apologize for creating the modern world" the Proud Boys (a name that sounds like nothing more than a group of four-year-olds who have cleaned up their toys or gone potty successfully, both major accomplishments in early child development of which one should *actually* be proud). Though the Southern Poverty Law Center has designated the Proud Boys as a hate group, McInnes denies this and has even sued the SPLC for defamation—a not-at-all-hate-group-y thing to do.

So by the time my barber held out his phone to show me a photo that I didn't want to see (though I didn't know just yet how *very much* I didn't want to see it), my heart was already sinking, sunk, hopelessly submerged. In the photo, Gavin looked drunk, wearing a robe that hung open like stage curtains to reveal his dick just chilling there. He and I had the same haircut. My barber and I had the same haircut. It was the worst imaginable version of "Who Wore It Best?"

At the same time, I couldn't deny I liked the haircut. It looked good on me. But what did it say about me that just by sitting in this chair, getting this haircut, looking like whatever I looked like, all of a sudden I appeared to be the type of person who'd be really pleased to see a picture of Gavin

McInnes, head of the Proud Boys, literally partying with his dick out?

LONG BEFORE GETTING a haircut somehow exposed me to Proud Boy dick, hair had always been fraught for me. When was it that I really understood the power of a decent haircut? Luckily I'll never forget, because *Terminator 2*, one of the greatest action movies ever, will always exist to remind me. For reasons which are lost to time, when I was about nine years old my mom took me to Supercuts, or whatever the Massachusetts even-more-off-brand-Dunkin'-Donuts-of-hair version was. Up until then, she had always been of the "We have haircuts at home!" philosophy, which usually led to me sporting a choppy bowl cut. She never actually put a bowl on my head and cut around it, but it was somehow as if she couldn't stop envisioning an imaginary bowl on my head and proceeding from there. And, as I'm sure you'll be very surprised to hear, the Scotch tape touch-ups didn't help my bangs at all.

So I wasn't going to waste this rare opportunity to get a real-ass professional haircut. When I sat down in front of the stylist, I held up a picture of Eddie Furlong in *Terminator 2*, a movie that was already out on VHS but that my strict Catholic parents were never going to let me see. Clearly a cool movie, I reasoned, so if I couldn't see it I wanted to *be* it somehow. Also I just wanted to look handsome. Also: much, much thinner. Finally, because all the kids in my class couldn't stop talking about *Terminator 2* while I was coming up conversational snake eyes, I needed this haircut to convince them beyond a shadow of a doubt that I, too, had seen this goddamn movie.

The stylist did her best. But when it was over, all I felt was disappointment. The cut itself seemed to be a success: A crisp part separated my hair into two asymmetrical lobes, one tucked behind my ear as the other hung over my eye. Unfortunately, ruining the whole effect was my same dumb face.

But even though the haircut didn't magically transform me into Eddie Furlong's even-better-looking twin, it actually did end up fulfilling a few of my outrageous expectations. On Monday at school I fumbled my way through a conversation about Arnold Schwarzenegger ("He's . . . a . . . nice . . . robot? And . . . was . . . *not* nice . . . before??"), and then one of the Joshes in my class—no less than the second-coolest Josh himself—told me "nice haircut."

Which is how I learned that haircuts could be magic. And this would have been a totally fine lesson if not for the fact that I was still a child with zero dollars who would have to beg his mother to take him to off-brand Supercuts again, which she generally wouldn't. But now that I knew transformation was possible, I couldn't go back. I had no choice but to fuck with my hair on my own.

I've never liked the way I look. First as a chubby kid, then a younger man with body dysmorphia, and finally the man I am now, I have wanted to look different almost my entire life. So I'm extremely here for anything that can help make that happen. And that's the thing, the dream, of a haircut, right? That somehow messing with this mess of dead cells that grows out of your skull can make your whole body—and thus your whole I-ness—look better, cooler, richer, whatever. If you could only figure out how to do it right.

Hair is so, so easy to fuck with, not to mention fuck up. That's why it's one of the first ways kids try to exert control over their appearance. By changing your hair, you can change yourself—subtly or drastically—in ways everyone will see, even if they've never seen you before.

Plus, you could do it for free. Hair dye could be shoplifted. Your best friend, Connor, could shave half your head. Your mother could pick you up after your friends invent a drink they call "weirdcore" (cheap bourbon mixed with Carlo Rossi and god knows what else), which led to your buddy Dave giving you a mohawk, and in the silence that fills the car as your mom drives you home, you could give thanks that she couldn't beat your ass and steer at the same time.

Terrible. Blonde. Tips.

Did I look like shit for the most part? Of course. But I was grateful for the chance—any chance—to look different.

My hair experiments paused late in high school, when I focused more on paring my body down in various aforementioned ways and stuck to the standard haircut, with short sides and a gelled front, that is exactly what you picture when you think of the phrase "white dude with brown hair." This was my status quo for years, until I moved from San Francisco to New York City in my late twenties. In sunny San Francisco, I had finally gotten to a place in my working life where I'd figured things out and didn't feel like dying—then I blew it all up to move to NYC during the worst winter the East Coast had seen in a decade, for a job that was exciting but *not* all figured out. I quickly gained forty pounds.

My fix for all this was getting one of the worst haircuts of my life: shaved to the scalp, except for a wide strip of long hair on the top of my head that was slicked back. Depending on your perspective this might not sound that bad, but 1) it was, and 2) no haircut exists in isolation; you have to see it on a specific person to tell what it's going to be, and on me it looked both stupid and mean. I don't know much about Pokémon, but someone saw a photo of this haircut recently and assured me that I looked exactly like a Pidgeot.

Getting a trauma haircut is a time-honored way of attempting to reassert control, of course. Unfortunately, it often results in you playing yourself, since during those times when you feel lost and in flux, deciding on a whole new hair-style is almost as ill advised as choosing whom to date. In both cases you make decisions based on an imaginary self, hoping against hope that both the self and the outside world will somehow contort themselves and thereby transform a wrong fit into a right one.

On a side note, nowhere was this more clearly shown than in *Avengers: Endgame*, which (accidentally or on purpose) does a deep dive into the myriad ways that upheaval and trauma can compel you to fuck up your hair. Like so: post-apocalypse, the two captains remained captain-y. Captain America shaves his beard to reassert control (and to hearken back to simpler, more winning times) and keeps his hair trimmed with a protractor, while Captain Marvel gets a not-too-dissimilar power cut, though with a little more swoop and flair on top. Black Widow chooses the path of neglect, letting her dye job grow out and keeping it in a sad multicolored braid. Hawkeye just stops giving a fuck about everything, as far as I can see—as there's no way he could sport whatever that is on top of *his* head and believe in a just and rational universe. Finally, Thor lets his beard, hair, and entire body go (and this, needless to say, I loved best of all).

I was now a patchwork of my San Francisco self, my New York self, my boy self, my man self, my responsible job-having self, my boozy fuckface scamp self—and although everyone else is of course similarly patchwork-y, I couldn't figure out how to make my outside cohere into something that made sense to me, that would make me satisfied to present myself to the world. But I wanted to.

So instead of doing what I'd always done before—rolling with the awful haircut, letting it grow out, then giving up and settling for basic, because at least basic won't let you down—I kept trying to look better.

EVERY BARBERSHOP I went to had a similar vibe. You know the kind: There was an explosion of them in the early aughts, and then they never really went away. The combs in the blue antiseptic water, a throwback barber pole creating a hipster aesthetic that says "We like old stuff, but don't worry—we're still cool." There's a bottle of whiskey by the register that welcomes you to take a shot as you settle up your tab. A flag, often American but without the current number of stars, hangs on the wall in a big wooden frame.

This isn't one particular barbershop, mind you. It's a lot of them. And I'm not gonna lie: That aesthetic is my shit exactly. Past shit with present shit, punk shit with old-dude shit, plus the fun of a bar, except unlike in a bar you look better when you walk out than when you came in.

I was drawn to the look and atmosphere of these barbershops—like *Terminator 2*, I kinda wanted them to be my life—and there were plenty to try out in NYC.

Which was good, because I had to try *so many.*

The quality of the cuts turned out to be the least of my problems. To my great surprise—because talking is the one thing I always think I know how to do—the main issue was the conversations *during* these haircuts. I would come in hopeful and fresh, sit down all ready to chat and get clipped, and then . . . time after time, it all went to hell; time after time, I was plunged into so many moments from the Telling on Oneself Hall of Fame that I started to wonder if there was something about me that made these dudes want to talk about the worst shit on their minds.

There was the guy who wouldn't stop talking to me about his failing relationship, even though everything he said made it pretty clear that he was the one fucking things up. I kept my mouth shut and reminded myself to mind my own business and stay in my lane.

There was the guy—the bunch of guys, really—who seemed to view the barbershop as a safe space for the airing of offensive views. You know the type—like a nineties shock jock who claims to "make fun of everyone." Sure, he makes jokes about his gay cousin, but he's an equal opportunity hater, he'll make fun of anyone (total coincidence that this "anyone" turns out only to be the marginalized/oppressed/etc.) and besides, it's his *cousin.* With this guy, I did notice some of the other barbers bristling at his comments—nobody liked what was coming out of this dude's mouth, but hey. It was the barbershop. The real talk spot. And they all had to work with him. I could leave if I didn't like it. And that's just what I did.

There was the guy who started showing me a video, composed of clips from security cameras and cellphones, of women being hit. "Because, you know, you're not supposed to hit women, but sometimes . . ." He let the words hang there. Waiting for me to laugh, or maybe to say something like "if they hit first." The haircut was almost done. I looked at him and asked him to turn off the video and finish up, please. I had someplace to be, I said. He rolled his eyes, put the phone down, and we spent the next five minutes in agitated silence. I walked home thinking about why I, someone who grew up in a violent household filled with domestic abuse, hadn't said more.

Finally, there was the guy who showed me Gavin McInnes's dick.

Being the captive audience at the men's evil bullshit parade nearly every time I sat down for a haircut sucked. What also sucked was that I wasn't just sitting and watching the spectacle go by—this was their way of holding a hand out, inviting me to jump on the float. I felt implicated, because somehow I was. One reason these men felt free to talk to me like that was I looked the part. The tattoos, the tight sides. I understand that if you took a photo of me and wrote "Alt-Right Poster Boy" underneath it, nobody would blink. Because of this, certain people sometimes speak more freely around me, when I truly wish they would do the opposite, and then go get bent.

The thing is, after years of working as a bouncer, I am not inexperienced with physical altercations and am pretty good at talking drunks down when they're being complete assholes. The other thing to know about me, though, is that . . . I'm polite. Too polite. Like my therapist recently described me as a "pathological accommodator" and the outrageous accuracy blew my mind. Like once I was at a book fair talking to some Scientologists without knowing it, and even after I realized that I was talking to Scientologists I kept the convo going for another twenty minutes because I didn't want to be rude, and it was only when they handed me a clipboard asking for my email and phone number that I got up the nerve to pretend to get a phone call and mouth "I've got to take this" at the Scientologists and shrug apologetically before scurrying away, my phone not having made a sound.

This politeness is a sickness. And yes, my therapist and I are working on it now. But I still have the politeness of my past to keep me up at night. Even as somebody who prides himself on living a life without much in the way of regret, I can honestly say that I regret every time I didn't speak up while I was sitting in those barber chairs. And sure, I could add something about how it's hard to disagree with someone when they're lining your beard up using a straight razor but that's weak and you know it and I know it. Full stop.

At the time, rather than deal head-on with any of this—pun intended—I took the coward's route and decided to grow my hair out. Long hair, no therapy, don't care! But you can't ignore your hair forever: That shit just won't stop growing. And you still have to do stuff to long hair to have it look good, a truth I was conveniently trying to forget, even as I began to look like a murderous drifter. Still, I probably would've kept it going for quite some time, except that I got a new job, and the new job was on camera and they were not down with the *Mindhunter* cameo look. I needed a haircut, and then I needed to keep getting that same haircut every couple of weeks, indefinitely.

AS SOON AS I walked into Badlands in Park Slope, Brooklyn, I knew I had found my place. It was not a barber shop but a salon, with a large rainbow flag in the window and a punk rock vibe. Not the bad kind of punk rock vibe where it's the same old jocks and bullies worshipping at the church of manly aggression only in slightly better outfits, but the good kind of punk rock vibe, where it's about being weird and mad and fun in whatever fucking way you want. It felt like home. When I slid into my chair, I was eye to eye with my stylist, who had a shock of bright, expertly dyed hair and gave off an impression, both literal and figurative, of sparkling all over. Her name was Rachael. As soon as she put the cape over my shoulders, she launched into a story that began, "Back when I was in the circus and lived in Louisiana . . ." By the end of my appointment, I looked sharp, and more importantly, I felt like not-an-utter-sack-of-shit. After forty-five minutes chatting with and learning all about the hilarious, interesting, kind person cutting my hair, I felt refreshed, peaceful, just . . . good.

For almost two years, I saw Rachael every two weeks. Though I no longer have a job requiring strict hair maintenance, I still go in whenever I need a trim. Rachael tells me about her pup Ru (unstoppably adorable), her bartender boyfriend (it's working out!), and her most recent adventures (someone is doing her twenties *right*), and I do one of my favorite things, which is to not say much at all.

A few months ago, I had an event coming up and needed to get my ears lowered—but Rachael was on vacation, so when I walked into the salon, I was paired with the one guy who works there.

Drew is white, tall, lanky, cool—which put me on my guard right away. But the more we chatted, the more the tension I hadn't even realized I was feeling drained away. Drew is from Ohio, and lived in Boston for a while before moving to New York, which led us into talking about friends back home, which led us into talking about talking to old friends. Drew said he'd been discussing privilege with his white friends back home, but hit on using the word "blessings" instead. He knew it wasn't a perfect match, but it had helped some people get used to the idea—after they'd been talking for a bit—before he substituted "privilege" back in. He told me that he's had more than one friend come around on the subject and discuss how they can now see themselves as privileged.

None of this is to say that all folks back home, wherever that is, are inherently more ignorant or less thoughtful and caring and knowledgeable—only that Drew and I, and countless others, had a lot of chances to be plopped into new environments among new people with new (at least to us) ideas and ways of thinking and being. We learned, we listened, we kept our mouths shut, we fucked up, and somewhere along the way we managed to show that certain kinds of conversations might not be wasted on us. The chance to grow like that is something you earn; it is also a tremendous gift, given to you by others with astonishing generosity, especially when you consider that they have no idea what they'll get back.

RECENTLY I WAS at a friend's house in L.A., and mentioned that I was working on this essay. On hearing Gavin McInnes's name, my friend got up and dug around in his closet until he emerged with a copy of the 2004 collection *Vice DOs & DON'Ts: 10 Years of Vice Magazine's Street Fashion Critiques*, a book I hadn't cracked in over a decade.

I opened it up. Over the next hour I took a trip down a very specific type of memory lane, one we might call What-a-piece-of-shit-I-used-to-be-as-evidenced-by-the-shit-I-used-to-find-hilarious Road. *Wheeeeeew.* It's not like I don't know that *Vice* was meant to be edgy; but the book wasn't just sprinkled with a few badly aged jokes here and there. It was nothing less than an artifact from another era.

Over time, cool does one of three things: It dies a rapid death, after which the corpse is interred in the tomb of the permanently uncool, where it remains. Or it may die a rapid death and then, twenty or thirty years later, come back to life and fight its way out of the tomb. Rarest of all, it lives forever. Rarely, because cool changes fast and it changes *hard.* So it was no surprise that the *DOs and DON'Ts* no longer seemed at all cool to me. They sounded more like some-one's shitty, horny, drunk dad talking over the TV while channel-surfing.

The real surprise? After rereading the book, I found it wasn't only *overtly* awful—it also contained more subtle awful-ness than I'd remembered, ultimately making it all the more awful and insidious and damaging. I went in expecting a plain old outrageous faceful of racism and misogyny, and got . . . well, yeah, a whole boatload of racism and misogyny, with much of it cloaked and buried and tempered in various ways . . . along with a whole lot of transphobia and fatphobia, which wasn't.

Gavin McInnes loved to give offensive compliments—to reference racist canards about Black penis size and Asian math skills while thumbs-upping people's outfits. They were Trojan horses with praise as the facade, because if you accepted the praise, you'd also need to engage with the horrible ideas woven into the praise as if they were worth considering, weighing, or even accepting. One page contained an image of some Nazi fuckheads at a rally, marveling at their dapperness and mastery of graphic design (and isn't that oh so very familiar?); the next image was of anti-Nazi protesters at that same rally. Both were DOs.

A brief interview at the front of the book highlighted McInnes's "both-sides-either-way-who-knows?" thinking, especially when he tried to answer the question of what makes someone a DON'T. He said something about how DOs don't try too hard, before acknowledging that sometimes it was random: "Often there's no difference between DOs and DON'Ts. It's just whatever works better." Occasionally there were too many DOs for a given issue so he'd turn them into DON'Ts, or vice versa.

I'm sure it would be telling to know which photos he was most willing to recategorize—and which photos were non-negotiably a DO or a DON'T—but it also doesn't matter. The devil was in his very shiftiness, his trickster quality. Was he praising or condemning? Was he mocking and moving away from hate, or speeding toward it? And he's still at it to this day. (Again, McInnes vehemently denies any and all allegations of being a racist or a Nazi, or of founding a hate group.)

This kind of stance is a hallmark of hipster racism, which had its prime in the early aughts. Hipster racism is, of course, just racism-racism, distinguished by the lie that we are now all so equal and copacetic that we can joke and laugh about racism and racist shit, and that the more one did so the more one proved this point, setting aside that there are those for whom life contains so many opportunities to laugh at others and so many fewer occasions to laugh at themselves; and the

fact there are those who are asked to ignore, damage, sacrifice themselves to laugh.

The McInnes of the *Vice* DOs and DON'Ts was slippery,
wrongfooted, unpindownable. But you can't joke about
everything and mean nothing forever. More than fifteen years
later, I believe he has shown us what he really means. The
mask became his face, or it always was, and it is the same face
worshipped and worn by so many people in this current
moment, that shifts at a moment's notice from troll to jester
to dapper dan but is recognizable by the hate shining out the
eyeholes.

WHEN I WAS turning thirty-seven I started growing my hair
out again. Less to do with any terrible experiences at barbershops this time around, and more likely an unwillingness to
face the fact that I was growing older. But even though I
might have had an issue with giving up my BMX or skateboard—and I did buy a ridiculous hat as a stopgap while my
hair was at an awkward stage, but also just because I loved
this dumb hat—I was so damn happy to be just-turned-thirty-
seven me.

Because at some point in my life—and this is something I
considered while flipping through my friend's copy of *Vice
DOs and DON'Ts*—a book that, at twenty-three, I thought
so important that I made room for it in the one bag I packed
for my move to San Francisco, three thousand miles across
the country.

That, by the way, was the first time I saw Gavin McInnes's
dick. I brought it all on myself. It was the early 2000s, and

Vice was the only magazine carried by the bar where I was working, and when the collected *DOs and DON'Ts* came out, it seemed to appear instantly in the bathroom of every twentysomething wannabe cool kid in the country.

Near the front of the book was a photo of Gavin McInnes that would have been nude except for a very fake-looking pair of briefs that had been drawn on top of him on the picture. But no need to worry about what you weren't missing: Marooned on a page near the back was an image of the exact redacted dick area, which you were instructed to cut out and glue onto the photo in the front. It was a joke, a joke on everything, a joke on the prudish publishers, a joke on an author making it very clear he wanted everyone to see his dick, and a joke on anyone who would go to the trouble of cutting and pasting the dick. A joke on anyone who didn't think it was funny and anyone who did. One last little edgy joke in a book filled with them. Or at least that's how it seemed to me.

So, yeah, to recap: When I moved to San Francisco, my copy of the book was in the one bag I took, which meant I'd made room for it, a little cutout of Gavin McInnes's dick removed from one page so it could be glued to another (because I was one of the idiots who *did* go to the trouble), carrying it and everything else I didn't know three thousand miles with me. Only to move three thousand miles back, years later, book and accompanying dick lost and forgotten until I sat down for a haircut and was reminded of that dickhead's dick all over again.

Remembering this book, and how hilarious I thought it was, made me feel shitty. It's hard not to try to immediately justify: "Well, a lot of people liked the book." "Well, he was joking, right?" "Well, it's not like I liked *all* the jokes."

Look. Not everything ages great, our own pasts most unattractively of all. When you look back over your history, I'm sure it's not just glimmering perfect accomplishment after glimmering perfect accomplishment. If it is, then . . . good on you and I wish you a happy life, but I personally wouldn't trust you as far as I could throw you (which, given the whole aging thing, isn't very far these days).

I enjoy spending time with folks who learn from their mistakes. Lord knows I have. But that's the thing. You have to take a person and look at the things they've done over the years. Growth isn't just saying, "Look, I've grown" or "Oh, I'm sorry." Growth takes effort. Growth takes time. Growth takes listening and learning, and then having those conversations yourself, like my barber Drew does. I've benefited from all of the people in my life, present and past, who have helped me grow by having those types of conversations with me. Who helped me take myself from places of ignorance, or not getting it, or not getting it seriously enough.

I know that educating people in this way can sometimes feel like explaining very nicely and patiently and calmly to the person who's just stabbed you—and who is still gripping the shiv as your blood runs down their knuckles—why they might want to consider not doing that. So of course I'm not saying that people must always educate others, especially when this responsibility so often is imposed on those bleeding from the deepest wounds.

But I cannot pretend that I'm not incredibly grateful to everyone who has ever taken the time to help me become a better person.

That's what angers me about organizations like the Proud Boys, who take advantage of the fact that these conversations are happening, who take advantage of the feelings spurred in so many young men by them—rage and confusion and mockery and hurt and fury—to say "You are good. You are right. This country, which was once built by you and for you, is now against you. Change it back." The Proud Boys and others like them tell these young men they are perfect just the way they are, which has the useful side effect of taking their anger and tripling and quadrupling it, until they don't remember how they felt before they chose anti-growth, anti-knowledge (both general and self-), anti-future, anti-people-not-laughing-at-the-exact-same-shit-you-do. It is poison to be so lazy and ignorant in your perfection, and it also sounds pretty fucking "snowflakey" to me. Because nobody's perfect.

To any young men out there who aren't too far gone, I say you're not done becoming yourself. You can keep growing. Growing, it turns out, is what this life is all about. Don't fear change—fear being only who you are right now forever.

And to anyone who has struggled with the things I am grappling with in this essay, I say have the uncomfortable conversations, even if they may lead to a scrape or two, or a falling out with your friends or family. Fuck your racist uncle. Or barber. Stop letting people have those ideas so comfortably, and stop forcing marginalized people to have those conversations on their own while you sit, politely quiet, telling yourself you're one of the good guys while you refuse to even get close to the heat, let alone jump into the burning building.

I'm grateful that I'm no longer the person I was. Of course, the person I was is still . . . me, and I remember him having his faults, but being not *all* that bad . . . but I'm not so invested in thinking that dude is so rad and unimpeachable that I'd fucking want to be him forever.

Thank god for the conversations that changed me, most of all for the people who had those conversations with me. And anytime I feel afraid to speak, to be rude or hurtful or overbearing, I need to remember that it's the only way I can really repay my gratitude. I can do for others what was done for me. Maybe it'll get me into a fight every now and then, or everyone will call me a stupid asshole the second I walk out the door or whatever else, but I'm a white, straight, cis guy with tattoos who doesn't have a shiv in his side, so what is the big deal, truly? For too long I failed to treat people as if what they said and did was something real to me and others; I failed to speak out. I'm not failing now; I won't in the future. But there will be so many other failures; some of them I'm sure are in progress already.

My Story

My parents were married when they had me, just to different people.

It's my opening line, when you ask to learn more about me. I sit back and wait for the nervous laughter—the reaction we all turn to when we don't know what to say. "A child of passion." I wink and smile. What a gift, to be born of two people who couldn't help themselves.

If we don't know each other well, that's all I give. Shift the focus of the conversation back to you.

If we get to know each other a little better, I might allude to a loud, dark childhood. I'll have written and published a few essays that do the same. Flashes of the past, but nothing more. Just enough that you know it wasn't pretty.

If we become friends, over the years I'll bring up stories that I've buried, ignored but not forgotten, taking them out from deep within the vault inside me, useful for its powerful lock and thick walls but all the more heavy because of them. These stories are about my mother and her sadness, my father and his coldness, and the affair that seemed to start it all. Not the affair they had together, which made me, but a later one. The nights of fighting in a house in the country, a house which gradually became so filled with shouting and violence and despair that when I was young I thought it must be haunted: haunted by spirits of sadness that had transformed my loving but scrappy family, warped it and changed it, somehow possessing us and turning us on one another, because what does a child know about the cold hard factual reality of how a family falls apart?

At some point, if we've grown close, if I consider you chosen family, I'll reward you by breaking down crying over dinner, detailing the pain. The suffering. The unimaginable confusion that comes when you, as a small child, are hurt by the people who were supposed to protect you. When you are put in the position, at the age of eight, of raising your mother, instead of her raising you. Coping through her suicide attempts and flashes of manic behavior. Sleeping in bed with her at night, the heated bricks from the base of the stove keeping us warm as she wept and said things to me that I was not supposed to know. Later, my father hitting me, not in anger, but after the anger had dissipated and there was nothing left but coldness. Coldness and intention. In the shower, his hands hammering down on my face and naked body along with the water, the shower curtain rod sometimes coming down on me too.

LET'S BE HONEST. Sometimes all of the above—the crying, the stories, the pain—might also happen if you and I have just met: if I know that we'll never see each other again. If we're two strangers at a bar, say, both of us looking for something to distract ourselves with. Swapping tales of sadness and defeat.

Then there are the partners in my life on whom I have leaned far too hard, when we've had a night or a weekend or a few days together and somehow I end up crying in bed, finally drunk enough to admit to myself that I can't believe two adults—two people I've come to understand couldn't help themselves, couldn't stop themselves from making enormous mistakes—would have let their own child down so heartbreakingly.

Other partners lived with me for years. For so long, the memories of abuse were kept hidden in my vault, unlocked only when I was drinking. You don't, I'm sure, need to be told how poor of a coping mechanism that was. Relationship after relationship crumbled under strange pressures, mysterious even to me. I thought I had everything under control, when I so clearly didn't. Still don't. But at least now I know. At least now I'm working at it.

My hope is that you'll take one thing away from all of this, maybe the only life lesson I've learned: Do not put off acknowledging your pain. Weeks turn into months turn into years, and those are years you will never get back. And they stack up, one on top of another, eventually becoming the structure and shape of your life. Unacknowledged pain? Refusing to work on yourself? Yes, there are consequences.

EVERYBODY MENTIONS HOW kind I am. They always have, even when I was a child. Later, as an adult, I got regular praise for being "polite" and "nice," though there were others, from time to time, who saw that kindness as weakness. Which . . . in a way . . . it may have been. But not in the way those people thought it was. It's hard to be anything but kind or nice when you've been raised on a steady dose of religion and abuse. The principle of turning the other cheek embodied in the physical act of turning one's cheek, the other stinging from your father's slap, water from the showerhead raining down on your body.

"You're so polite."

"Thanks, it was beaten into me."

Not the response anybody wants to hear. So I don't give it. See? Polite.

THE THING I would never tell anyone, not even close friends, was the time I struck back.

The time I, still in middle school, so filled with anger—and now knowing that my childhood should not have looked like what it had looked like for the past four years—lost control.

My mother's anger and my own is rising as we fight, as we now do every day; she takes a swing at me, and I, for the first time, realize that I'm bigger. The way I push her back over the sink and wrap my fingers around my mother's neck, and repeatedly say, "I could kill you right now."

I could kill you right now.

I could kill you right now.

I could kill you right now.

She looks up at me and I, for one of the first times in my life, look down at her. Both of us stunned, both of us horrified.

The abuse has yielded more abuse. The anger is there, has always been there. But now the lesson of violence has been fully learned.

How could this house not be haunted?

I REMEMBER MY mother and me in the gray house in the country, not long after we moved from Boston. Her parents watched over me when she had to work. I always had plenty of chores to do around the farm, followed by the smell and feel of sheep shit and horse manure, the geese that always hated me. My mother's parents were from New Hampshire, the Granite State. And so were they. Granite. Only later in life did I get to see cracks in the hardness: my grandfather, telling stories of stolen cars taken for joyrides, much like me in my youth, although I never raced the cars down frozen rivers the way he did. Once, not long before he died, I saw him in nothing but his underwear running around and around the outside of the house in the middle of a raging thunderstorm.

"Try to do that as often as you can," he said to me after, getting dressed in the kitchen.

"Do what?"

"Run around naked in the rain." And he winked. I realized in that moment where I had gotten at least some of my wildness from. He died while I was doing my work with the Free Burma Rangers. I didn't make his funeral, but years later I was grateful that I was spared having to watch the cancer take him: that my last memory is of him strong, upright, and

joyful, standing naked and dripping wet on the yellow lino-
leum floor of my grandparents' kitchen.

But that all came later. When I was a child they were cold
and unforgiving. Like I said, granite. And they lived right
next door. I remember my mother going to their house, once
a week, in the evening. I'd sneak over and sit right below the
windowsill, listening to them slowly pick my mother apart.
"We told you this would happen," they would intone, as my
mother cried helplessly. They didn't like her life choices and
they weren't afraid to tell her, or me. Which hurt, as I was
very much one of those choices.

YEARS LATER I would find out that my grandmother was a
cruel woman because people had been cruel to her. I'd always
thought I was the descendant of immigrants on each side of
my family, just a generation or two back. Irish. But in my
twenties I learned that my grandmother was a direct descendant of Josiah Bartlett, a signatory of the Declaration of Independence and a governor of New Hampshire. But you
wouldn't know that. Being a daughter, and not a son, she
didn't get any of the Bartlett farm, which was distributed
between her brothers. There was no money or land left for a
daughter. No inheritance. So she, in her anger, married a
charming, tall, *poor* man, and started a farm of her own.

You think your family is one thing, then begin to learn so
much more about it, until it eventually becomes another. You
think you know who you are, but there's always so much more.
I'd always thought I was a poor child raised in a homeless

223

shelter in inner city Boston. And I was—but I am also a bastard prince of New England.

I REMEMBER THE day my father introduced me to the woman he was having an affair with. Every few weekends, my mother would drive me back into Boston. Back in the city I was happy. The excitement, the energy—it was still there, along with the memories of better times.

My happiness made me feel guilty. In the haunted gray house out in the country, my mother was becoming a ghost herself, whereas I was temporarily freed, excited to be away from the dark forests and wide, sad fields surrounded by rock walls that had long ago lost their magic, the very picture of the blandly terrifying all-white town in the Shirley Jackson story that my father had made me read at—you guessed it—far too young an age.

It was just a day in the city, but we spent it laughing and smiling.

"Do you want to meet Katherine?" he asked.

She lived in Cambridge, her husband a wealthy man. Apparently my father was still chasing the dream of marrying rich, even while being very much married. They'd met at school. Sound familiar? I remember thinking how cruel my grandparents were to judge my father so harshly. But now that I'm an adult, well—I can see that they had their points.

Back then, all I knew was that Katherine smelled nice and that she wasn't crying, and that she gave me Oreos and cold milk and played basketball with me. Her house was big, and there were no bugs in it, at least not that I saw. She showed me her new child, a baby, and I held him.

When my mother came to pick me up she asked me how my day was and I, forgetting my father's request that I keep the day between us, told her everything. Joyfully, I explained what a happy, lovely day I'd had—trying to hold on to those feelings of warmth, because it had been so long since a day had felt normal. Since I'd had a day I wanted to share with my mother.

She became so still, despite driving the car. She took a turn, heading the wrong way down a one-way street.

"Tell me more," she said tightly.

I realized then that everything had changed. Things were already bad, but somehow I had managed to make them even worse. I had done what my mother and I tended to do when we were alone in her car. I'd said too much.

THE YEARS THAT came after were not easy. I have a memory of my mother trying to stab herself in the stomach with a knife as she collapsed in front of me, crying. The knife sliced through her thick green Champion sweatshirt as I tried to pull her arm away from her body, yelling "No!" over and over again.

There was the time I found her, a teetotaler out of respect for my father's sobriety, on the floor with an empty bottle of vodka and an empty bottle of pills. There was the time she locked herself in the basement, screaming that she was going to kill herself as I did my damnedest to knock the lock off, my small body bouncing against the door again and again.

In the fourth grade I switched schools and left my bus driver Trudy and the new friends I was trying to make, solely so that I could keep an eye on my mother at the school where she taught. She spent every morning and every afternoon crying as we commuted together—tears rolling down her cheeks and I so very scared that she would drive us right off the road, wrap us around a telephone pole, end it all as she kept threatening to do.

I told no one. The pain was our pain, ours alone. She lost the teaching job at the end of the year, but not before I got into a fistfight on the playground, my front tooth knocked out by a foster child named Patick, his nose bloody as I slammed a basketball into his face with all my might over and over again. The violence was growing, encompassing me, reaching out from me to touch others.

AFTER THAT YEAR, my father finally found a job outside the city. My parents decided to try to make it work.

On the day he moved out of Boston, we packed both our cars up and then drove them out to the country, unpacking them at the gray house and going back into the city to do it all over again. My father tried to lose us on the highway: he sped up, figuring that my mother wouldn't give chase with their child in the car, but of course she did. She was convinced that he wanted to try to go see Katherine one last time, and it turned out she was right. I don't remember how that day ended—all I remember is how we sped down the highway, weaving through traffic, me, petrified, hands gripping the sides of my seat.

My father would bring more instability into the house, not less. The ghosts that lived there had already become so strong, and he would only help them grow stronger.

THE FIGHTING HAPPENED every night, my mother unable to forgive my father for his misdeeds, my father never seeming to understand that he was the villain. Once, back in Boston, before he'd come to live with us permanently, I remember my parents returning home from a trip: some outdoor excursion, maybe canoeing in the wilderness, or backpacking in the White Mountains. They were trying to patch things up, and at first it seemed like they had succeeded: they came back exhausted but happy. They picked me up from wherever I had been staying (most likely my half-brother's house), and once we'd all come back to my father's apartment, my mother hit Play on the answering machine. Katherine's voice filled the room.

All traces of happiness dissipated instantly. In its place were screams, accusations, the answering machine wrenched from the table and thrown across the room.

In her message, Katherine had mentioned a detail from a poem that my father had sent her: something about both of them being able to gaze up at the same moon despite being in different places. Real corny shit. Could she have known that my father would return from his trip, walk into his home with his wife and son in tow? Did she have any inkling that the message she had left was one that we would all have to hear?

My mother grabbed me by the arm and pulled me all the way down the stairs from the ninth-floor walk-up. We drove the eighty miles home to North Central Massachusetts. She cried the whole way, telling me about STDs, how my father could kill her with his infidelity. I knew, even then, that she didn't really know what she was saying. I knew that in her darkness she was forgetting to treat me like the child I was. But that didn't help me to shut out what she was saying. I can still hear her now.

MY FATHER MOVED in with us but continued traveling to Boston to take classes. He'd gone from teaching religion to working in Catholic school administration, and he would eventually become a principal and receive his doctorate from a prestigious college. He worked hard. Still does, always will. He was focused on living a better life than his parents had, a better one than the life he'd known as a child. On becoming greater than the sum of his parts.

He continued to see Katherine. I sometimes wonder if my father was more in love with the lives these women led than he was with the women themselves—with their lives, and with the attention they gave him. Katherine the well-to-do wife, living in Cambridge. A good neighborhood, a good house. A new baby. She was never going to leave that family to be with my father. But maybe that didn't matter to him. Maybe what he really wanted was simply to get close to her kind of life, a life of wealth and status and ease, in the hope that some of it might rub off on him. Lord knows I've done the same kind of thing in my own ways, getting a scholarship to boarding school and befriending people whose lives seemed so sweet and soft to me that I couldn't believe they weren't happy for every moment of it every day.

Eventually the affair with Katherine ended. I'm not sure when, because it doesn't matter. All of the damage had long since been done.

NOW, WRITING THIS, I can see that I held my mother responsible for it all, even though so much was clearly my father's fault. *His* inability to change or to keep his promises. *His* actions worming their way into my mother's mind and making her go mad.

As a child I remember dreaming of running away with my mother to Mexico, where we would rob banks to survive. I had never been to Mexico or anywhere else, really, but I knew from cowboy movies that it was a good place to go if you wanted to make a run for it. All I wanted was for the fighting to stop, for the yelling to stop. For us to make our great escape.

I never told my mother about this fantasy, and I regret that now. Maybe it would have made her feel less alone. All three of us were so lonely in that house.

One day when I was ten my mother sat me at a picnic table in a park and said, "I'm thinking that your father and I should get a divorce." The lightness my heart felt in that moment. It was already dusk and turning darker, but inside I was all brightness and elation. How had it taken them so long to figure this out? I remember telling my mother that I thought it was a good thing, and then we drove home.

The divorce never happened. I never heard it mentioned ever again, save for that one special, lovely evening. Soon I was back to fantasizing about us in my mom's car, heading down to Mexico.

AFTER YEARS OF fighting and violence, my grandparents growing colder and colder to us as we proved ourselves to be the fuckups that they'd always suspected us of being—my parents' fights often exploding out of the house and into the driveway or backyard (years later, old neighbors who lived a quarter of a mile away would contact me after reading one of my essays to say that they often worried about me living in that loud house)—things took a turn. A good one, improbably. My father, who was now living with us, saw my mother's pain in a way he hadn't been able to back when he was in the city. One day when I came home from school, I found my mother after another suicide attempt with alcohol and pills. My mother was put in a hospital, her visit paid for by the state. She was gone awhile—a couple of weeks, maybe close to a month. She was prescribed new pills, and things slowly began to improve. My father's job was going well.

My parents were getting better, and I was getting worse.

BY AGE TWELVE I had a job at the local country store at the center of town. I knew money meant independence, and so I started trying to make whatever money I could, however I could, which included stealing packs and eventually cartons of cigarettes from my boss, then selling them as loosies at my middle school. I made older friends: high schoolers with cars who drank and did drugs. I became their energetic little mascot, getting held upside down over kegs in the woods as I guzzled foamy beer, taking whatever pills they threw my way just to see what would happen. They drove me to the malls, where I became so good at shoplifting that I made a game out of stealing at least one item from every store in the place, no matter what they sold. I called it "Around the World": It started with you having to first steal a bag for storing all your other items (shoes, CDs, earrings, water guns from the toy store, even lingerie from Victoria's Secret).

At the age of twelve I had a seventeen-year-old girlfriend and most of my friends drove trucks. By thirteen I was doing mushrooms and acid, had smoked heroin-laced joints on more than one occasion, and in general knew how to get my hands on weed and alcohol—sometimes by breaking into homes, taking nothing more than any bottles we could find and, sure, maybe a few dollars if we happened to come across them. I started selling weed to a friend's mother who was also having a rough couple of years. Eventually I ended up taking keys from one of the houses we had broken into: not a residence, but a summer house. Some folks from the city had these secluded places up in the hills. Inside, dust had accumulated on their tables and chairs, on the bottles we'd already helped ourselves to. And then the keys, taking a stolen car for a joyride, which was the exact perfect word for it. The joy, the *thrill* of driving fast in a car that was not your own. A car that was not my mother's.

After the last four years, I felt as if my parents had no right to dictate my behavior, to try and raise me, and at times

I wondered if that was how they felt too. But they had no choice but to try—after all, what else can you do when you've kept your marriage together against all odds and obstacles, and are dealing with the stresses of a very good and promising new job, and things feel like they might just come together . . . except now your own kid is the one who's starting to screw everything up?

Whenever I was at home, things got aggressive and violent. None of us knew when someone was going to explode in anger. Sometimes it was me. And sometimes I was the one being punished, almost at random, for the many things I'd already done, or for what it was assumed that I had yet to do. More and more I began to avoid going home. The moment I walked through that door, I knew I was most likely entering some kind of hell, so why try?

I spent more time at my friends' places, especially at Connor's, whose mother was always kind to me. She let me smoke her GPC cigarettes and mostly left us alone, having plenty of her own problems, but always made sure that there was food in the fridge and that we felt loved. She had two sons and always called me "Number Three." For years to come, many of us regularly ended up at Connor's house, his mother becoming a mother to us all.

BACK THEN, I wondered if my parents had stopped loving me. They hadn't, of course. They didn't hate me, either, but I was a child, and it was confusing not knowing what to do with love that arose out of fear and sometimes turned into violence. Actually, I'm pretty sure that anyone of any age would be confused by this. My mother, too, was still grappling with her sadness. Sometimes a movie or a song on the radio would set her off, and soon yelling and crying and wailing would fill the house.

Once, when my father was out of town, my grandmother came over to our place—something that almost never happened. It was winter and I was out starting the car, warming it up and scraping the ice off the windows. As my grandmother approached, I got into the driver's-side seat and, through a scrim of slowly melting ice, watched her meet my mother at the front door of the house. They began to argue almost right away.

"Get out! Get out! Get out!" my grandmother shouted. She was trying to kick us out of the house—her own daughter, who had clearly been struggling. I watched as my mother transformed into the child of a parent who loved her but had failed her, and was continuing to fail her in countless ways. I would only come to fully understand their history much later in life. Hell, partially understand at best, if we're being honest.

We're all still working on something. My father's father had beaten him with sticks, with belts. Everybody has a past. Everybody has a story. We are all sinners, forged out of others' heat, sinning and sinned against. There are very few saints in this world. And very few monsters. Most of us are a mix of both.

I REMEMBER ONE blessedly calm night in our backyard in the country. I remember feeling that night that as much as I missed Boston, I loved the country too. Both feelings, I realized, could be true at once. The wide-open spaces and trees and stone walls and swimming holes. The ability to ride my bike wherever I wanted, no matter how far. My mother and I sat in the backyard, as all around us lightning bugs began to emerge with the setting of the sun.

"It's a sin to kill a lightning bug," my ma said to me, and we just sat there and watched them. A moment of peace.

BECAUSE THIS IS not just the story of a difficult childhood and of all the ways I reacted against that difficult childhood while genuinely believing that I was acting of my own accord. It's also a story about what came next.

THE YEARS PASSED. Slowly but surely, I figured out how to live my life, how to find the things I loved and how to get good at those things and even be able to admit to myself that I *was* good—that I was allowed to feel proud of myself. Occasionally, at least. Though I'd found the problem of my family unsolvable, I got out of the house at the age of fourteen during the school year, and by sixteen I had a summer job that allowed me to be out of the house year round. By the time I was in my early twenties and living in San Francisco, my parents had made it through some unemployment scares and job changes and were starting to find some success of their own. The next decade was one of upward mobility for me—and funnily enough, the very same was true for my parents.

It's odd to feel this way now, when I consider the fact that my parents divorcing was something I used to yearn for—literally pray for—but I'm happy that they ultimately stuck it out. Things change. And now, decades later, as they grow older, I feel lucky that they have each other. That they've grown together and matured together. That they figured things out. Not everything, of course. They're not perfect. But I like that they're together. Still complicated, yes, but not alone.

SO MUCH HAS changed over the years. One of the most important changes, for me, has been watching our family grow. I knew from a very young age that I wasn't going to have kids myself. But my half-sister (father's daughter) now has two sons, and my half-brother (mother's son) has both a son and a daughter. I love all of them, my siblings, their partners, their little ones, very, very much. I moved back to the East Coast to be closer with them. I already knew I was gonna be the weird uncle, which I am, of course. But I didn't want to be the weird uncle who was three thousand miles away.

What none of us expected—and trust me when I say I've had this conversation with both my brother and my sister—what *none* of us expected was how my mother and my father would step up as grandparents. Both of my siblings have said how surprised, amazed, and pleased they are that my parents have become such reliable, dependable, and ever-present guardians.

I watch them holding their grandkids—so gently, so tenderly—and I know there must have been a time when they held me like that. But now I'm an adult, and I get to watch those kids get older, and to see how my parents always have time for them, always have love for them. As if my parents are getting a second chance, and they refuse to screw it up. It's a wonderful thing to behold.

It's also a peculiar feeling to be jealous of a three-year-old.

NOT TO SAY that everything is perfect now. My brother and sister understand that they, and not our folks, rule the holidays; I take pleasure in it, and I'm sure they do, too. All these grandparents, all these families with all these divorces and complications—well, if they want to see the kids during the holidays, they've got to show up to my brother's place on Thanksgiving and my sister's place on Christmas. Those are the rules. No time schedules, no whose day is which. If you want to eat and see the grandkids, you must show up, and yes, you might be sharing the table with the ex whom you divorced not-so-amicably back in the early eighties, but the kids are running the show now and their kids are the prize. Show up or don't. It's up to you.

This is always hardest on my mother, whose mental health has greatly improved over the years, but who still has the lingering anxieties that I can recognize so clearly in myself now. Just this past Christmas, in my sister's stately home outside of Boston, my mother pulled me aside.

"Can you see?" she asked.

"See what, Ma?"

"My missing tooth."

"What?"

She pulled her lips back, exposing a missing molar. All of a sudden I grasped what was happening: My mother was nervous that the other grandparents would be able to see her missing tooth when she talked.

I reassured her. "No, Ma. It's fine. Way in the back. Nobody can see that. It's fine, Ma."

She sat quietly for a moment. We were in my sister's lovely furnished basement: We hadn't turned on the lights and the sun had gone down. The room grew dark with almost no warning.

Then she spoke. "You know, it's your dad that knocked it out." She got up and walked out of the room. I sat there alone and wondered lots of things. Like when? Ten years ago? Twenty?

We carry our wounds and our scars and those things we are now missing long after the damage has been done.

Or worse, what if it was not that long ago at all?

"ARE WE GOING to be arrested for child abuse?" my father asks me at one point, when we're talking about my writing. He isn't joking, but he isn't *not* joking either. It's his Irish way of asking, "How bad is this book going to be?"

It's a fair question. They're in their seventies now. Retired. Living out their golden years, years that they worked hard for. How would you feel if someone took all of your worst moments from more than twenty-five years ago and put them in a book? Ignored all the good times, of which there were many, and highlighted every tragic moment, unable to put aside their resentment? Unable to do the one thing the religion you raised them in taught them to do: forgive?

THAT SAID, MY father has never apologized. For a few years, when I was in my late teens and for a bit of my twenties, he took a break from his sobriety, though he is now sober again. In that time we went to Scotland, where we visited distilleries of scotches and did another thing my father loves to do: walk. It was a wonderful trip, especially considering that we had spent most of the past decade avoiding each other.

In a bar, late at night, I asked my father, "Do you ever still talk to Katherine?"

"No, no. Of course not," he replied, taking a sip of the dram of Oban that sat in front of him. Then he smiled, and added, "But I do hope she shows up at the funeral."

We both laughed. Soon he would be sober again. And while I personally might be that rare case—a child who liked his alcoholic father more when he drank—I've heard from my mother that those years had not been easy. That it was a slippery slope, each slipup or mistake leading to others, and that she was relieved when he put the bottle down again.

I realize, even to this day, that I'm harder on my mother than I am on my father. I can't explain it. All I know is that every time I hear about a family moving out of the city and heading to the country I get nervous. That is how my parents lost their minds. That is when, in my child's memory, they went from being parents I knew and loved to being parents I no longer knew and hated. That is where the ghosts found them, and that is where they found me, too.

I SIT AND watch my parents playing with their grandkids. They are so good with them, and for a moment not only do I feel the pang of wishing that my childhood could have been the one that these children will have—I also find myself wondering why my own grandparents hadn't been kinder to me. On my mother's side, that is. My father's mother had loved me and spoiled me. Christmases in her New Bedford home were trashy and joyful, heaped with wonderfully, wastefully torn wrapping paper and cheap plastic toys, as opposed to the carefully unwrapped socks and wrapping paper folded and reused at my mother's parents' house. I used to treasure those moments with my paternal grandmother, and even the story of how my father's father, after holding me for the very first time, content that he had a grandson, stepped outside to smoke a cigarette and promptly had a heart attack, dying with his back against the family truck. (I have since been told that it was not immediate, and some months passed between him holding me and his dying, though he did have a cigarette between his lips and he was lying against a truck when they found him.)

I talk to my therapist about all of this and so much more. I tell her that I want to forgive my parents.

"I think you should start by talking to them about what happened, before you get to trying to forgive them," she tells me. Then she notes that everything I've written about in this book, which is to say a large part of my identity, is just me trying to communicate my pain to them. My stories. A child, crying and acting out, hoping to make his parents understand what's happening. What's been happening for so, so long. A child who wants to know, once and for all, that he wasn't a mistake.

I haven't had that conversation yet, but I'm hoping to. I haven't forgiven them yet, but I try to.

I try. I try. I try.

ACKNOWLEDGMENTS

This book would not have been possible without the tremendous efforts of Nancy Miller, Charlotte Sheedy, Alice Sola Kim, Meredith Kaffel Simonoff, Kelly Farber, and John Wray.

Thank you to Jason Diamond for dreaming up the title *Dirtbag, Massachusetts* while on a road trip to Boston where we stayed at a rundown motel in the shadow of Fenway Park.

Colossal thanks to my blurbers, Marlon James, Min Jin Lee, Kiese Laymon, Mira Jacob, Alexander Chee, and Emma Straub.

I deeply appreciate John Darnielle granting me permission to use his lyrics for the epigraph in this book, and Mikael Kennedy for allowing me to use his photography.

Heaps and heaps of gratitude to my early readers, Saeed Jones, Teddy Goff, Chloé Cooper Jones, Jami Attenberg, Scaachi Koul, and Cathy Berner, who all took turns holding my anxiety.

I'm indebted to everyone who helped edit the numerous essays that eventually made their way into this collection, including Steve Kandell, Karolina Waclawiak, Rachel Sanders, Sandy Allen, and Marisa Carroll.

I will always have deep appreciation—and admiration—for the entire team at Bloomsbury, including Myunghee Kwon, who made such a beautiful cover for this book. Also Patti Ratchford, Tara Kennedy, Marie Coolman, Nicole Jarvis, Suzanne Keller, Jennifer Choi, Harriet LeFavour, Gleni Bartels, Katherine Kiger, and everyone else at the company.

ACKNOWLEDGMENTS

To everyone who has been supportive of me over the years. To everyone who has been forgiving and understanding. To anyone who has helped me grow, and to all of my friends, who are far too numerous to name here. For that I consider myself eternally lucky. Thank you.

I am forever grateful to Dr. Jenny Kaufmann, with whom I continue to do the work.

Lastly, thank you to my family. Many people with stories like mine don't even get recognition from their loved ones, let alone understanding. I love you all very, very, very much.

A NOTE ON THE AUTHOR

ISAAC FITZGERALD appears frequently on the *Today Show* and is the author of the bestselling children's book *How to Be a Pirate* as well as the coauthor of *Pen & Ink* and *Knives & Ink* (winner of an IACP Award). His writing has appeared in the *New York Times*, the *Guardian, The Best American Nonrequired Reading*, the *Boston Globe*, and numerous other publications. He lives in Brooklyn.